Saint-Laurent, Manitoba

Saint-Laurent, Manitoba:

Evolving Métis Identities, 1850–1914

Nicole St-Onge

2004

Canadian Plains Research Center
University of Regina
Regina, Saskatchewan S4S 0A2
Canada
Tel: (306) 585-4758
Fax: (306) 585-4699
e-mail: canadian.plains@uregina.ca
http://www.cprc.uregina.ca

Library and Archives Canada Cataloguing in Publication
St-Onge, Nicole J.M.
Saint-Laurent, Manitoba : evolving Métis identities, 1850-1914/Nicole St-Onge.

(Canadian plains studies, ISSN 0317-6290 ; 45)
Includes bibliographical references and index.
ISBN 0-88977-173-1

1. Métis–Manitoba–St. Laurent–History. 2. Métis–Manitoba–St. Laurent–Ethnic identity. 3. St. Laurent (Man.)–History. I. University of Regina. Canadian Plains Research Center II. Title. III. Series.

FC126.M3S23 2004   971.27'200497
C2004-905924-6

Printed and bound in Canada by: Houghton Boston, Saskatoon
Cover image courtesy La Societe Historique de Saint-Boniface (MD 317-33-01 pht)
Cover design by Donna Achtzehner, Canadian Plains Research Center
Index prepared by Elizabeth Bell, Pinpoint Indexing
Chapter page image: Métis guide "Marion," Provincial Archives of Manitoba (N11969)
We acknowledge the financial support of the Government of Canada through the Book Publishing Industry Development Program (BPIDP) for our publishing activities.

CONTENTS

To my husband
Philippe A. Beaudin
and my daughter
Colette G. St-Onge

ACKNOWLEDGEMENTS

I N THE PREPARATION OF EVEN A RELATIVELY SHORT WORK such as this there are always many who must be thanked. The Social Sciences and Humanities Research Council of Canada provided funding for the first version of this manuscript through a doctoral studies grant. My parents, Denis and Jeanne St-Onge, provided moral and financial support through the long years of graduate studies. The University of Manitoba and the Collège Universitaire de Saint-Boniface helped bring forward the project with both material and technical support. The University of Ottawa aided in the completion of this work with both a developmental leave and several small grants. Professors such as Doug Sprague and Louise Sweet from the University of Manitoba, colleagues and friends such as Avis Mysyk, Micheline Lessard and Jacques Barbier, among others, provided enthusiastic support during years of intellectual musings and doubts.

This work could never have seen the light of day without the foresight of Gilbert Comeault of the Provincial Archives of Manitoba, who in the 1980s spearheaded the Métis Oral History Project. These interviews, along with those done by Father Guy Lavallée for the Michif Language Committee, are at the heart of the book. A very special thanks goes to all the people of Saint-Laurent and Saint-Ambroise who agreed to be interviewed for either of these projects. All the staff at the Provincial Archives of Manitoba, the National Archives of Canada, the Centre du Patrimoine (Saint-Boniface) and the Archives Deschâtelets (Oblates of Mary Immaculate, Ottawa) also receive heartfelt thanks.

I am also indebted to Les and Linda Branconnier, and to Manon Lalande, for their genealogical expertise and computer mastery in creating the charts and graphs found within these pages. They did admirable work with rather opaque instructions from my part. Some of the photos in the text were uncovered thanks to the efforts of my *ma tante et mon oncle* Thérèse and Roger Hébert. Finally I would also like to express my gratitude to the Publication Coordinator Brian Mlazgar and the editorial committee of the Canadian Plains Research Center for their enthusiastic support of this work during the publication process. My appreciation also extends to Roger Turenne, who allowed the use of his photograph of Saint-Laurent fishermen out on the ice as an illustration for this work.

Nicole St-Onge
Ottawa, October 2004

MAPS PREPARED BY DIANE PERRICK, CANADIAN PLAINS RESEARCH CENTER

Top: Oak Point, as it is located on Lake Maniboa.

Bottom: Oak Point, Saint-Laurent, and other settlements of the time.

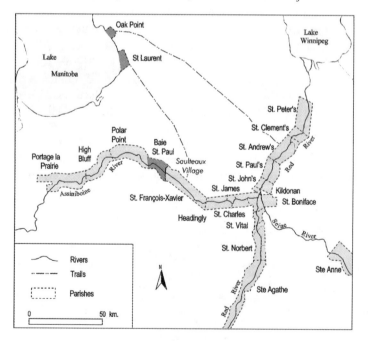

Introduction

SAINT-LAURENT DU LAC IS A SMALL MÉTIS COMMUNITY on the southeastern tip of Lake Manitoba. Traditionally, its people, history and development have been viewed as typical of the Catholic Métis parishes of the Red River Settlement. This study contends that Saint-Laurent differs in three fundamental ways. First, prior to 1880 the Métis of Saint-Laurent led a more diversified life than the Métis specialized in bison hunting. Second, their self-identification as Métis did not follow clear and steadfast "rules" as has been argued in past studies. Third, economic variations within the lakeshore community had been growing from 1850 onward and produced complex social interrelationships that affected self-identity.

In the past 20 years many studies have shown that Métis identity and history in the North-West are very diverse and complex.[1] As early as 1987, Jennifer Brown argued that the term "Métis" had come to be "applied in countless different ways, ranging from the highly specific to broadly inclusive."[2] She noted that recent writings dealing with the Métis reflected

> that variability, although "Métis" is increasingly generalized in popular writing to all people identifiably of mixed Indian-European descent, some with little regard to whether they themselves merit or would elect that designation in either social or political terms.[3]

J.R. Miller, in a 1988 historiographical essay, echoed Brown's sentiments. In his view, the broadening of meaning of the term "Métis" was a necessary step in coming to a fuller understanding of frontier societies linked to the fur trade. He commented that "Red River myopia" had, to some extent, previously limited the interpretation of the "heterogeneity of mixed-blood experiences in different topographic and economic zones of the continent."[4] Miller argued that the growing, continent-wide research on dual-descent populations should be further encouraged. He also posited that this research needed to be sensitive to the reality of class structures within mixed-blood populations and to class-based links between the Métis and the larger world. Only then could the histories of dual-descent populations be truly understood and appreciated.[5]

The need expressed by Brown and Miller to be sensitive to the diverse experiences of the peoples of mixed ancestry on the North American continent is a real one. However, this author goes further and argues that even in the traditional areas of Métis studies a historical reinterpretation is required. "Red River myopia," or the "bog of Red River" as it was defined more recently,[6] has not only skewed the histories of dual-descent communities outside the Red River Settlement but has also prevented a complete appreciation of the peoples traditionally labelled "Red River Métis." What follows is a contribution to the ongoing debates over internal socio-economic and ethnic variations at Red River through the prism of a single small settlement; one albeit situated on the fringes of the Colony but still considered by researchers as fully integrated to it.

This study begins by examining the early history of the Métis community of Saint-Laurent. Between c. 1850 and 1867, neither the resident trading families nor, especially, the itinerant lakeshore Freemen Métis fit the traditional definition of

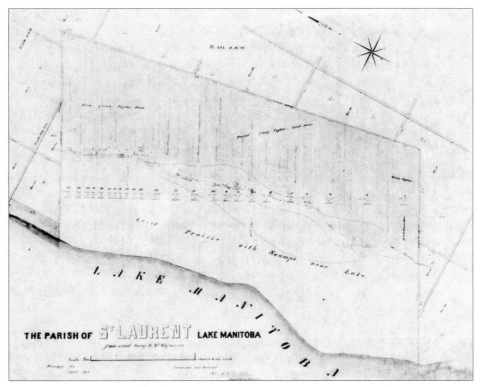

PUBLIC ARCHIVES OF MANITOBA (PAM) N4560

Map made by William Wagner of his survey of Saint-Laurent in the early 1870s.

the bison-hunting Red River French Catholic Métis. Their livelihood came from a mixture of the subsistence activities that resembled those of the Saulteaux population, with which they were closely allied, and the commercial production of dried or frozen fish, pelts and salt. In lifestyle and economic pursuits they resembled much more the residents of Father Belcourt's "Sauteux" or "Saulteaux Village" (also known as Baie St-Paul), situated on the shores of the Assiniboine River, than the inhabitants of the other French Catholic Red River parishes. Chapters 1 and 2 of this study demonstrate both the surprisingly close historical and familial ties between Baie St-Paul and Saint-Laurent, and their enduring distinctiveness from the other Red River settlements. Great caution has to be used in attempting to define the social, economic, and ethnic parameters of Red River "Métiness."

Chapters 3 and 4 examine the arrival of new Métis families—economic refugees or opportunists—from the older nearby settlements. They came between 1868[7] and 1881[8] to the lakeshore mission. The Métis families that settled in Saint-Laurent during these years were from parishes situated along the Red River or from the bison-hunting settlement of Saint François-Xavier. By and large they were relocating to the south shore of Lake Manitoba—a traditional fishing spot—due to a difficult social and economic juncture related to the decline of the bison hunt and repeated disastrous crop failures. It is during these same years that the Catholic Church, represented by the Oblate Order of Mary Immaculate, affirmed its presence in the area by transforming the mission into a parish and exerting ever-increasing economic, social and moral influence on its inhabitants.

These families—Boyer, Chaboyer, Daigneault, Goulet, Carrière and others—differed in terms of their lifestyle and world view from both the merchant and Freemen families. More sedentary and endogamous—few engaged in long-term marital relationships with the nearby "Indian" population—they were also much more obedient of the dictates of the Oblates and, with the decline of the bison hunt, much more interested in agricultural pursuits. The newcomers showed little interest in trading or freighting along the lakes. They oriented themselves towards commercial fishing and mixed or dairy farming. They never had the economic or cultural ties to the Lake Winnipegosis Saulteaux and Métis population enjoyed by the merchant and Freemen population. Their economic *point de mire* would continue to be the core of the colony. Though all these families—merchants, Freemen and fishermen-farmers—considered themselves to be "Métis," social and economic distinctions amongst them would endure into the 20th century.

Chapter 5 documents the process by which this socio-economically stratified lakeshore community restructured itself after 1881. This restructuring came to be interpreted locally in ethnic terms due, in part, to the arrival of Québecois and Breton migrants. The rise of social Darwinism in the late 19th century was also a contributing factor. No new social classes were created, but existing differences and economic marginalization were reinterpreted using the ethnic identity—i.e., the degree of "Métiness"—supposedly produced by the mixture of races as a key explanatory factor.

What is striking about the history of this settlement, and about Métis history in general, is that by the 1950s well over half of the descendants of the 18th and 19th-century Canadian-European workers and local Native women did not perceive themselves, and were not perceived by others, as Métis or "Half-breeds."[9] They had fully integrated into so-called white society. Any obstacles encountered in their daily lives were not the products of a racist ideology (which they themselves often espoused). When "Métis" were defined by society at large, some allusion to Indian ancestry was made and physical characteristics were noted, but, in fact, these were given social significance *only* because of the lifestyle led by the individuals. In the 20th century "Métis" came to be synonymous with being poor, unschooled, living in a shack, or engaged in a variety of seasonal employments—persons not very submissive to authority who formed a significant part of Manitoba's reserve labour force. Once an individual or a family was enmeshed in this cycle of poverty, a theory of racial determinism was invoked: Métis were poor because of inherited characteristics. This work concludes with the argument that if a family once defined as Métis became prosperous, its white parentage was emphasized until the day, at least in the Oblate parishes, when it would merge with the French-Canadian element. By the second decade of the 20th century, being Métis in Saint-Laurent was as much a function of one's class as it was of one's ancestry and culture.

CHAPTER 1

Saint-Laurent

B Y THE LATE 1820S, SEMI-PERMANENT SETTLEMENTS existed in the Saint-Laurent and Oak Point areas of Lake Manitoba, where winter fishing and trading with fur trappers could be carried out.[1] These communities were never completely self-sufficient. Their formation stemmed from a need by a segment of the Métis population for access to foodstuffs and other country produce for family consumption. Also, these Métis needed access to sources of goods, such as fish, salt and furs, to be bartered to the Hudson's Bay Company (HBC) or other suppliers for needed imported goods. Thus, the southern shore of Lake Manitoba became the rallying point in spring and autumn for Métis involved either in the production of salt or in freighting and trading ventures on Lakes Manitoba and Winnipegosis. Most of these early lake dwellers also combined such activities with buffalo hunting in the White Mud River district and, increasingly, autumn or winter fishing on the lakes.

The first indications of relatively permanent dwellings being erected in the Saint-Laurent area date back to 1818, when it was determined that the settlement of Pembina was in American territory. The Hudson Bay Company officials and the Catholic clergy urged Métis families settled at Pembina to relocate north of the border. The majority of families that moved settled, initially at least, on the shores of the Assiniboine River. A few, however, chose to settle directly at Fond du Lac (Saint-Laurent) where good fishing existed.[2] A few more families permanently relocated there when flooding of the Red River in 1826 forced a large number of Métis to winter at this fishing site. By the time a Catholic mission was founded in 1858, there were 30 to 40 households residing intermittently at Fond du Lac.[3] Interestingly, Giraud sees the majority of these Saint-Laurent Métis as being of "Freemen" or *hommes libres* descent.[4] That is, the Saint-Laurent dwellers were from a group of families at the margins of the Red River Settlement and its core Métis community. For a time at least, they would successfully resist HBC Governor Simpson's post-1821 efforts to concentrate the part-time trapping, hunting and wage-labouring "mixed" population in the Settlement.

These Saint-Laurent Métis are part of a phenomenon studied by authors such as Heather Divine and John Foster. Descendants of French Canadians and their mixed-blood offspring, they moved away from regular employment with the fur companies and chose the role of socio-economic intermediaries. In a time-honoured fashion they practised, with the help of their extended families, limited subsistence activities (hunting, fishing and, very occasionally, gardening) but mostly they focussed their energies on entrepreneurial activities. These activities centred on their role as social and economic brokers. They served as conduits between the fur companies they had worked for, and were familiar with, and the extensive Native kin network they acquired through wives or mothers.[5]

These early south-shore dwellers located themselves beside a key trading route ("trail") which followed a slight rise, at some distance from the lake, separating the old meadow land of the lake flat from the higher wooded land of the interior. The community was therefore conveniently located for fishing from the lake, haying in the meadows, and for gathering firewood and lumber from the forest. They were also in a strategic position for bartering and exchanging with the local HBC post

Traders and hunters in a Métis settlement in Wood Mountain. A visual example of the written description of Saint-Laurent-Fond du Lac, c. 1872.

(situated in Oak Point) or with people using the trail.[6] Fond du Lac had a good natural harbour, where barges coming from the north could discharge their cargoes. It was the main transfer point between lakes Manitoba and Winnipegosis and the Red River Settlement. The first families to settle seasonally in the area were at least as interested in trading as they were in fishing commercially:

> The site of the Pangman-Chartrand-Sayer homes was a strategic point for the Métis and the Saulteaux from the north of the lake, who came and went on the prairie. These people spent the winter in the forests and marshes of the north, hunting and trapping. In the spring, they came down the lake, on huge barges, with oars and a sail, headed first to Fort Garry, and then for the buffalo hunts on the plains. They came with their large families, their ponies and carts and all their chattels. [...] When they returned from their buffalo-hunts, loaded with pemmican and dried meat, the blissful hunters came back to the same place, where they stayed ten days, fifteen days, and sometimes a month, before returning to their winter quarters Sometimes as many as fifty tents were pitched along the lakeshore. Then there were rounds of feasts, dances and games, and very often liquor also, and then there were quarrels and sometime bloody fights.[7]

According to letters in the correspondence of Mgr. Provencher, by the mid-to-late 1820s a certain number of Freemen Métis were choosing to spend an increasing amount of time in the area of the Red River Settlement. Though they hunted buffalo for home and trade purposes on a yearly basis, they kept returning to their river lots. Some attempted agriculture but in those early years this was an uncertain proposition for climactic, political and market reasons. More and more Métis in the 1820s and 1830s practised autumn or even winter ice fishing on lakes Manitoba and Winnipeg and at the *Grande Fourche* of the Red River (situated in American territory).[8] In these places a plentiful supply of sturgeon, white fish and goldeye attracted a large population.[9] Fishermen and their families originating from the banks of the Assiniboine River would congregate at Oak Point on the shores of Lake Manitoba. They would use nets to catch fish that they then dried, smoked or froze depending on the temperature. They would haul their fish on ox- drawn sledges back to the Settlement once the snow arrived.[10] These Métis would remain in the Red River Settlement over Christmas to exchange their goods, renew social ties, and engage in some New Year's festivities. Some combined further fishing with muskrat trapping in the spring. Occasionally these fishing Métis chose to remain away from the Settlement for the whole winter and simply bartered directly with the free traders, as in Saint-Laurent, rather than making the trek to the trading posts.

In the 1850s at least four key extended trading families—the Pangmans, Sayers, Lavallées and Chartrands—had representatives either in Saint-Laurent or settled around the Oak Point HBC post. In both Oak Point and Saint-Laurent other trading families, such as the Delarondes and the Monkmans, were present but they were not as visible or as fully settled in the 1850s. Other families also spent various amounts of time in the area. Non-fishermen who faced adversity in their own economic pursuits took up fishing on the shores of Lake Manitoba quite frequently in the decades between 1820 and 1870.[11] For example, in 1847–48, a drought destroyed most of the crops at Red River. In the years 1855–57 the crops were rained out. Bison hunting would also fail, as in the years 1838, 1840, 1844, 1855, and both the hunting and the crops failed in 1867 and again in 1868.[12] The existence of plentiful hay pastures near Lake Manitoba also attracted people who could winter their animals while still engaging in autumn and winter fishing. The growth in the importance of "commercial" fishing tied to salt manufacturing, trading for some, and trapping, hunting and gathering for others, is notable from the mid-century onward.

From the little information extant on the non-trading Métis devoted to the exploitation and exchange of fish, life was marked by seasonal displacement. When fishing failed in one area the people simply moved. This was not an unusual pattern of Métis behaviour in the transitional middle decades of the 19th century. Authors such as Gerhard Ens argue that the pemmican economy had reached saturation point, with the HBC having finite needs and fixed prices. Controversy over the Métis right to trade independently resulted in open confrontation and, more importantly, a new market was opening up for bison robes at the same time as bison herds were receding farther and farther west. More and more Métis families who had moved to the Red River were choosing to return to the old *hivernant* lifestyle of wintering on the plains. They hunted herds to supply the American bison robe market. Though they did return to the Settlement more or less regularly, they did not reside there for long periods. Ens argues that for some Red River Métis, this was a time when attempts to lead a more settled agrarian lifestyle lessened because of the opening up of lucrative alternatives.[13]

As the fishing Métis' ties to mercantilism strengthened and production for exchange grew (as the demand for dried and frozen fish increased), a segment of the Lake Manitoba Métis chose the Saint-Laurent and Oak Point areas as their home base. But, at least up to the 1870s, several of these fishing Métis families would occasionally spend part of the winter bison hunting in the White Mud River valley (eastern slopes of Riding Mountain), much to the chagrin of the Catholic missionaries.[14] Yet the overall tendency for many seems to have been to gradually abandon the chase and to undertake ice fishing on a larger scale. With the large herds receding farther and farther west these families would eventually have to choose one or the other pursuits. However, displacement along the edges of Lakes Manitoba and Winnipegosis for fishing, trapping or trading purposes remained common well into the 20th century.[15]

Closely associated to fishing was the production of salt which developed, to a small degree, within the framework of the fur trade. A Catholic missionary, G.A. Belcourt, described in 1840 the salt-making activities of Métis families wintering on the shores of Lake Manitoba. They exploited these *salines* to manufacture salt for sale to the traders or directly to settlers in Red River[16]:

> Leur saline (près de Baie des Canards) consiste en une source d'où ils prennent l'eau salée pendant les gros froids d'hivers et alors la réduisent en sel en peu de temps par l'ébullition. Un homme a quelques fois fait 100 minots de sel dans son hiver; or ce sel se vend ici 10 chelins le baril c. à d. plus d'un chelin le gallon. Il y a beau-coup de saline du côté de la Baie des Canards ce sont des endroits pretés ou il ne pousse point d'herbes environnées d'épinettes ordi-nairement; en marchant dans une saline on remarque une extrême fermeté de sol qui est couleur de cendre. Pour peu qu'on y marche, les souliers de cuir mous, qui sont les seuls que l'on porte ici s'y percent; de manière que ceux qui font du sel ont le soin de s'attacher aux pieds une semelle de bois. Ceci n'a lieu que pour préparer la saline avant les gelées car ils font d'avance des fosses et des réservoirs où ils doivent puiser leur eau dans l'hiver temps auquel ils n'ont plus besoin de semelles de bois.[17]

> *Their salt works (near Duck Bay) consist of a water source where they take salted water during the coldest days of winter. They transform this water into salt by boiling it for a short time. A man can produce up to 100 bushels of salt in one winter. This salt is sold for 10 shillings a barrel, that is, one shilling a gallon. There are many salt flats around Duck Bay. These are prairie-like areas where no grass grows, usually surrounded by pine trees. When walking in a salt flat, one immediately remarks on the*

PAM N14806

Brine Spring at Monkman's Salt Springs, Lake Winnipegosis, 1889.

> *hardness of the ash-coloured soil. If a person walks on the salt flats for any*
> *length of time in moccasins—the usual footwear of this part of the*
> *country—they will end up piercing them. Those who produce the salt wear*
> *wooden soles tied to their feet. This problem exists only before the frosts when*
> *preparing the salt flat for winter production. At that time, the salt produc-*
> *ers have to dig trenches and reservoirs where they will collect the water they*
> *will draw from during the salt making. In the winter they no longer need*
> *wooden soles.*

Métis families from the Saint-Laurent and Oak Point area seem to have been actively involved in salt manufacturing.[18] Henry Youle Hind writes in his 1858 expedition notes:

> We met here [Waterhen River], also, a freighter's boat, in the
> charge of a French half-breed, who, with his family, was returning
> from Salt Springs to Oak Point, with about twelve bushels of salt.
> We exchanged a little tea and tobacco for ducks and fish.[19]

The Saint-Laurent area appears to have been a key transit point in the commerce of salt. In the same letter quoted above, Father Belcourt noted that no trading house existed in Duck Bay even though it was a good hunting and fishing area.[20] People with goods to trade waited for the itinerant traders or made their way to Fond du Lac. One salt producer and a *notable* of Oak Point was Paulet Chartrand (born at Duck River).[21] According to Father Morice, Paulet was engaged in the manufacture of salt in 1861 when he killed a neighbour in self-defence. According to documents relating to the history of Saint-Laurent, local Métis were selling their salt in the late 1850s for $2.50 per 60-pound bag.[22] Obviously, choosing a lifestyle not dependent on the bison robe trade did not mean a lack of integration into the market economy.

A secular priest erected a chapel at Fond du Lac in 1858, but by 1860 the Oblates of Mary Immaculate were fully in control of the mission. The Oblates were interested in the area because of the attraction it held for the Métis, whom the Oblates wished to Christianise or re-Christianise. Métis involvement in the hunt, the exploitation of the salt springs and their trading activities forced them into a semi-nomadic lifestyle, yet they consistently came back to the mission area where good fishing grounds and trading possibilities existed.[23]

There are no archival documents suggesting that much agricultural activity occurred in the area prior to the early 1860s. As Sprenger notes, farming was barely a viable occupation (in terms of both output and market demands) in the heart of the colony, let alone in the Interlake "hinterland."[24] In fact, the Saint-Laurent mission developed at a time when the agricultural sector was in decline in the more established parishes.

The earliest archival documentation listing the four extended families mentions, first, Pierre Pangman Jr. (born c.1815), from Pembina, who was married to Mary Short (b. 1820) of White Horse Plain.[25] He was the son of the Catholic Métis Pierre "Bostonois" Pangman Sr. (b. 1794)[26] and "Marguerite" or "Marie" [Wewejikabawik], a Saulteaux woman. Mary Short was probably the daughter of James Short, a Protestant Orkneyman married to Betsy Saulteaux, listed in the censuses as an Indian. Pierre Pangman Sr. had worked early in his life for the North-West Company, wintering in the Lac Winnipeg, Athabaska River and Red River areas, and had in fact travelled to Montreal in 1819, the year of his father's death.[27] He would settle in the Grantown (Saint-François Xavier) area of the colony after the 1821 merger of the North-West Company with the Hudson's Bay Company. In the 1840 census Pierre Pangman Sr. would be listed as owning a house, a stable, four horses, an ox, two carts, and a canoe, cultivating two acres and employing one servant.[28] The 1843 census listed him as cultivating six acres. Besides Pierre Jr., two other of his children, Marie and Marguerite, would marry and move to the Saint-Laurent mission.[29]

Pierre Jr. and Mary (Short) Pangman had eight children who lived to maturity (see insert, Pangman genealogical chart). The first four were born in the parish of Saint-François Xavier and the remaining four were born, or at least baptised, in the Saint-Laurent mission. Though most members of the Pangman family were spending part of the year in Duck Bay by the 1860s, they returned to Saint-Laurent on a regular basis.[30] Pierre and Mary Pangman are listed in a census for the parish of Saint-Laurent done during the 1868 famine. The family is listed as having seven

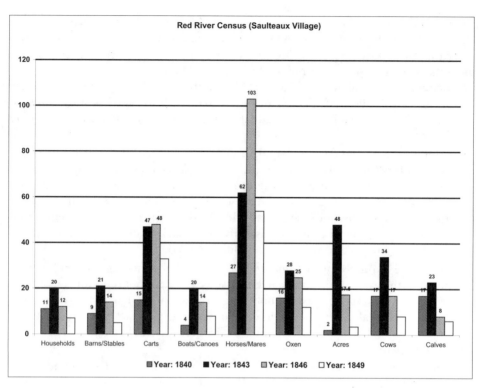

Red River Census (Saulteaux Village)

	Households	Barns/Stables	Carts	Boats/Canoes	Horses/Mares	Oxen	Acres	Cows	Calves

Year: 1840   Year: 1843   Year: 1846   Year: 1849

members, two of whom were under the age of 12. They are listed as having no horses or oxen, and possessing only a cow with her calf. They had not harvested a crop in either 1867 or 1868. In fact, the surveyors listed them as being "indigent." This is a far cry from the relative affluence of Pierre Pangman Sr. 20 years earlier. Interestingly, Pierre Jr.'s is the only Pangman family listed in the entire 1868 Red River census. Perhaps the other members had chosen to stay out on the plains or in the northern part of the lakes during these years of general misery. Again in the 1870 census, Pierre Pangman and his wife would be the only Pangman family listed for the Lake Manitoba area. The Oblates of the time noted that the children of Pierre Pangman Jr. were Cree-speaking.[31]

Also residing in the area by the 1850s were six brothers and sisters, children of Joseph Paul Chartrand and a Saulteaux woman called Louise Mazinakkamikak (see insert, Chartrand genealogical chart).[32] The last three were born in the Lake Manitoba area prior to 1830. Oral tradition states the Chartrand family originated in the "north." Certainly they had extensive ties in the Duck Bay area before 1850. For example, Oblate sources note that, in the summer of 1843, Father Darveau set out from Duck Bay for The Pas accompanied by Pierre Chartrand, "a Métis." It was also "the Chartrands" who were put in charge of building a chapel at Duck Bay.[33] However one of the eldest sons, Paul Chartrand Jr., married to Josèphte Cadotte, is listed in the 1843 Red River census as residing in the Saulteaux village[34] with eight children, a mare, two cows and a cart. Many of the founding families of Saint-

Laurent appear to have resided in the Saulteaux village as opposed to the more established Métis parishes. Giraud described them in particularly unflattering terms:

> Plusieurs familles enfin, attirées par la ressource de la pêche vivent misérablement le long de l'Assiniboine, à l'écart des colons de Grantown, étrangères au travail de la terre, attendant seulement la saison propice pour la grande chasse ou pour l'hivernement : pour l'hivernement surtout, car elles ne peuvent figurer active-ment dans les expéditions collectives, faute de posséder des char-rettes ou des chevaux de course, ce capital indispensable aux chas-seurs dans lesquels les métis du Cheval-Blanc, comme ceux de Pembina, investissent la majeure partie de leur avoir.

> *Several families, attracted by the fishing potential, lead miserable lives along the Assiniboine, apart from the Grantown colonists, strangers to agrarian work, waiting only for the time of the great hunts or for winter-ing. Mostly for wintering, for these families cannot participate actively in the hunts having neither carts nor fast horses, indispensable capital in which the Métis hunters of the White Horse Plains, as those from Pembina, invest most of their wealth.*

Comparing the effect of this Saulteaux village to Saint-François Xavier, Giraud had the following to say:

> Le contact de l'indigène y était plus direct que dans la colonie de la Rivière Rouge, soit par le voisinage des tribus nomades des plaines, soit par l'existence, à proximité immédiate de la colonie du Cheval Blanc, de la mission indienne de Saint-Paul des Saulteux, qui réunit pendant quelques années un certain nombre d'Objibwa et plusieurs métis d'origine canadienne assez proches de la vie primitive pour se confondre en fait avec les indigènes.[35]

> *The contact with Natives is more direct here than within the heart of the Red River Colony, partly because of the nearby nomadic tribes of the plains and partly because of the proximity, immediately next to the White Horse colony, of the St-Paul Saulteaux Indian mission, which for a few years has brought together a certain number of Objibwa and many Métis of Canadian origin leading such primitive lives as to become indistinguish-able from the Indians.*

Despite Giraud's unflattering opinion, as a group the children of Joseph Paul Chartrand appear to have been relatively affluent, with only Isabelle Chartrand, married to Pierre Richard, figuring on the indigent list in 1868.[36] One of Joseph Paul Chartrand's grandchildren, the son of Paul Chartrand Jr., was Paulet Chartrand, an important salt-maker in the colony in the 1860s. The habits and movements of some of the siblings, and their children, illustrate well the closer identification of these "lakeshore" Métis with the fur-trapping Native population as opposed to the more settled Métis of Red River.[37] This indicates, as in the late 1850s, their very nebulous understanding of Catholic dogma and the sectarian Protestant-Catholic divisions. The parish chronicles recount an incident that occurred in 1858:

> During the missionary's [Rev. Mr. Gascon] sojourn here, the Michel Chartrand* already referred to, arrived one afternoon from Fort Garry accompanied by two English Half-Breed Protestants. The whole three were strongly under the influence of liquor and of course high-minded "Touch me not." Chartrand approached the priest and said "Father I want you to baptise these two Protestants [for] they are going off on a voyage of two years." The priest replied that he would not without first giving them the necessary instructions... This did not at all please Monsieur Chartrand as he considered himself a big man and one that should not be refused under any circumstances. He then said to the priest in a most angry manner; at the same time swearing "get out of my house 'Passez à la porte' and leave from here."[38]

This incident (among many) illustrates how the traditional English-French and Catholic-Protestant divisions were not in force for the lake-dwelling segment of the Métis population. Christian dogma in general did not have a strong hold on the lake dwellers.[39] For example, some members of the relatively wealthy,[40] well-travelled Chartrand family led a lifestyle unusual, as far as the records show, for most Red River Métis but perhaps not the "Indian" trapping segment—which caused endless scandal and shock for the Oblate missionaries. Two brothers, the already mentioned Michel and his brother Baptiste, were both contributing to the maintenance of two wives. The first official wife was considered a Métis, the second, from the northern shore (or Lake Winnipegosis), was considered Indian. In 1862 Baptiste Chartrand (Opishkwat), besides being married to either Louise or Mary Stevens, was having children with an "Indian" from the Duck Bay area:

> Je viens d'arriver à la Pointe de chêne sur la barge de Pierre [Chartrand]. Demain, si le temps le permet nous ferons voile vers la Baie des Canards ensemble sur la barge de Paulet [Chartrand]. Sur ces deux barges seulement, il y a neuf familles dont quatre n'avaient pas coutume d'hiverner à la Baie des Canards. Je viens de baptiser un enfant de Baptiste Chartrand ... je l'ai trouvé dans sa tente avec ses deux femmes qu'il emmène à la Baie des Canards. [?] sa légitime consent quoique avec peine à le suivre encore une fois. Elle pense qu'il va renvoyer l'autre femme à la Baie des Canards.[41]

---

* Michel Chartrand was one of the sons of Paul Chartrand born in 1824. He is variously listed as married to Marguerite, a daughter of Pierre Bostonois Pangman, born in Pembina in 1832, and Sophie Napakisit/Flatfoot.

I have just arrived in Oak Point in Pierre [Chartrand's] barge. Tomorrow, if the weather permits it, we will sail towards Duck Bay, together in the barge of Paulet [Chartrand]. On these two barges alone there are nine families of which four were not accustomed to wintering in Duck Bay. I have just baptised Baptiste Chartrand's child... I found him in his tent with his two wives whom he is taking to Duck Bay. [?] his legitimate wife consents with reluctance to follow him there one more time. She believes he will repudiate his other wife once in Duck Bay.

In fact, Baptiste Chartrand would be linked to at least four women in the course of his life; two were French Métis, Marie Chaboyer and Genevieve Robert, and two were considered "Indians," Mary and Louise Stevens. There is some overlap between the births of these four women's children, born both in Saint-Laurent and in Duck Bay. Baptiste's younger brother Michel (Otchakwe) Chartrand also had two wives in the 1860s:

Michel Chartrand était chez lui avec Marguerite [Pangman*] et son autre. Il m'a dit qu'il allait rejeter pour toujours sa Sauteuse. Hier il a rempli sa parole et je lui ai permis de venir à la Chapelle. Ce qui me fait craindre un peu c'est qu'il tient a voir de temps en temps le petit que cette misérable lui a donné ce printemps. Il ne consentira jamais dit-il a voir ses petits garçons parmi les sauvages, il se croit obligé de les surveiller de près.[42]

Michel Chartrand was at home with Marguerite [Pangman] and his other wife. He told me he would reject forever his Saulteaux woman. Yesterday he fulfilled his promise and I allowed him to come to the chapel. What worries me a bit is that he insists on seeing from time to time the boy this miserable women gave him last spring. He says he will never consent to seeing his boys amongst the Indians, and he believes he has to keep a close eye on them.

These two excerpts illustrate well the fluid position of the "salt-making, fishing, trading, Freemen" segment of the descendants of Natives and French Canadians (or other) in the North-West. Their traditions and mores seem to derive more directly from the older trading elements either from the Great Lakes, the North-West or the Saint-Louis fur trade than those of the Saint-François Xavier and the Saint-Norbert bison hunting and farming elements. None seem to have worked formally for the HBC after the original eastern voyageurs and prior to 1870. They were Cree speakers[43] but identified quite closely with the neighbouring Saulteaux population. They continued (or replicated) the Great Lakes tradition of marrying into the local (in this case Saulteaux) tribes, with whom they were exchanging goods, while still maintaining a "Métis" household. But, as the second excerpt indicates, they nevertheless considered themselves distinct from the Native trappers to the point of refusing to let the "Indian" wife's family solely raise the children.

---

*   Daughter of Pierre "Bostonois" Pangman and Marie Wewejikabawik.

The two Chartrand brothers, members of the Pangman family, along with other families mentioned by Father Simonet, were apparently uncomfortable with the changes heralded by the Oblate fathers in the 1860s and 1870s. They withdrew farther north to the Duck Bay area where they pursued a more "traditional," and lucrative, life. Perhaps it was not so much "retreating" as following the receding frontier of a fur-trade economy within which they were able to make a comfortable living based on a variety of pursuits. In any case, they continued to have close family and business contacts with the Saint-Laurent and Oak Point area.[44] Two families with which they would have business and kin ties were the Lavallées and the Sayers.

Another extended family to take up residence at Fond du Lac prior to the arrival of the Oblates was that of Jean-Baptiste Lavallée (b. 1795, Isle à la Crosse) (see insert, Lavallée genealogical chart). He was the son of Ignace Lavallée (born c.1760, died Lake Manitoba, 1836), a French-Canadian North West Company voyageur from Sorel, and of Josèphte Cree, listed in the census as an "Indian." Jean-Baptiste's wife was Louise Ducharme (Métis, b. 1805, Fairford), the daughter of Antoine Ducharme (b. 1780, Saint-François Xavier[45]) and Josette Richard (b. 1787, Saint-François Xavier). In the 1843 Red River census, Jean-Baptiste Lavallée is listed as a resident of the Saulteaux village and as being the owner of a house, a stable, an ox, two carts, and as having two acres under cultivation. In the same census, Louise Ducharme's elderly father, Antoine, is listed as owning, again in the Saulteaux village, a house, a stable, a horse, two mares, two carts, a canoe, and of also cultivating two acres. Antoine and Louise Lavallée had six children who lived to maturity, many of whom were born in Saint-Laurent. During the 1867–68 famine the Lavallées were one of the extended families listed as "non-indigent"[46] (they harvested 75 bushels of potatoes in the autumn of 1867 and 12 bushels in 1868[47]). Between Jean-Baptiste and the four other Lavallée heads of family they possessed nine horses, three oxen, six cows and seven calves.[48]

The Lavallées had links to most of the other trading families of Fond du Lac. Antoine Lavallée (Jean-Baptiste's son) is listed in the 1870 census as married to Isabelle Chaboyer (b. 1848, Lake Manitoba). Her parents were Louis Chaboyer (b. 1803) and Louise Chartrand.[49] Again in the 1843 census, Louis Chaboyer is listed as owning three mares, a bull, two cows, two calves and as residing in the Saulteaux village. Another son, Jean-Baptiste Lavallée Jr., was the husband of Josèphte Ducharme (b. 1841, "Métis").[50] She was the daughter of Louis Ducharme (an American Métis born in 1818). Louis' parents were North West Company voyageur Nicholas Ducharme and Julia Deschamps, born in 1823.[51] A third son, André Lavallée, was married to Elise, a sister of Isabelle Chaboyer. Obviously the Lavallée, Chaboyer, and Ducharme families were closely connected, whatever the exact kinship ties.

The last and most difficult to document of the four founding families of Saint-Laurent to be described here is that of Guillaume Sayer (son of Guillaume Sayer[52] and Josèphte Forbisher) and his wife Catherine Pangman.[53] The son of a prominent free trader in the Red River area,[54] Guillaume Sayer Jr. established himself in Saint-Laurent in the 1850s at a time when he was already in the pelt trade on the shores of Lake Manitoba.[55] This family's struggle with the company to continue his illicit fur trade on company territory embodied Métis efforts to diversify their economic activities and reduce their dependence on the HBC. By 1870, Sayer and his four sons were residing intermittently in the parish (or at least were not there at the time of the census[56]). There was, however, a Sayer family residing in Oak Point. The elder Oak Point Sayer was Jean-Baptiste Sayer, born in 1800 at Île à la Crosse. He was married to "Marie" or "Marguerite," born in 1790 at Fort Francis and listed as an "Indian." Unfortunately the census does not identify Jean-Baptiste's father. His son was John Sayer, born in 1840 at Swan River and married to Suzanne Chartrand, born in 1847 at Lake Manitoba and daughter of the salt-maker Paulet Chartrand. Their children are listed as having land claims in Saint-Laurent and Oak Point (behind the river lots), as did the Lavallées and some of the Chartrand offspring. The relationship of the Oak Point family to that of Guillaume Sayer is unknown, though it is quite possible that Jean-Baptiste Sayer was Guillaume Sayer Sr.'s brother.

The exact points of origin for these four extended families—the Pangmans, Chartrands, Lavallées and Sayers—cannot be fully ascertained. Through the genealogies only the Pangman family had demonstrable ties to the Dakotas. However, according to religious sources recounting folklore, *all* the early families to settle in Saint-Laurent came from points northwest of Red River, spending time in the Pembina area before it was deemed to be American territory. Two families, the Pangmans and the Sayers, did reside during the 1830s and 1840s in the Grantown area. Both families owned livestock and Red River carts and their *point de mire* was quite clearly the bison hunt and trading activities, though they did each have two acres under cultivation. The Chartrands and the Lavallées settled for a time in Father Belcourt's Saulteaux village. They also had Red River carts and livestock but no acreage. As noted earlier, several of the later arrivals also would come from *village des Sauteux.* In the late 1840s and early 1850s the original four families appeared to have gradually relocated to Fond du Lac. Local folklore states that the Chartrands were a family from the "North," presumably Duck Bay. The birthplaces of the family elders (such as Île à la Crosse) indicate that the North-West is a more likely point of origin for some of the families, although the Dakotas may well have been used as a wintering place prior to relocation on Lake Manitoba.

The composition and activities of the four "founding" families of the Saint-Laurent-Oak Point area are interesting. None of the four elders or their sons seems to have worked (for wages) for the HBC between 1821 and 1870. The only possible exception is a Baptiste Lavallée, who signed a three-year contract at York Factory to be a *milieu et hivernant* for the HBC. This man could easily be Jean-Baptiste Lavallée. Their activities appear to have been confined to commodity production or independent trading (perhaps also freighting with the Chartrand barges). Some documented individuals, such as Guillaume Sayer and Paulet and Michel Chartrand, were quite successful. Their ties to the Native fur-trapping element were extremely close. The HBC had been concerned for many years about the trading activities of these Lake Manitoba peddlers.[57] Some of the lakeshore

Métis were in a position to engage in trading year-round.[58] From letters written by the missionaries, one gets the impression the common language spoken was Cree,[59] with Saulteaux added when sons (or husbands) married into the tribe.[60] Yet a certain differentiation was maintained between the two groups (the Cree-Métis that began arriving in the 1820s and the lakeshore Saulteaux).[61] Nevertheless these lakeshore Métis, compared to the Red River Métis who were developing increasingly distinct dialects, customs and traditions, seemed more comfortable speaking a Native language and residing near an "Indian" population.

It is perhaps not all that surprising that the families establishing themselves at Fond du Lac seemed more "Native"; after all, many were originating from the Saulteux village founded by Father Belcourt. Eventually the Saulteux village would transform itself into the settlement of Baie St-Paul, but the perception of its inhabitants being somehow more closely linked to the local Native population would remain well into the 20th century.[62] According to ecclesiastical sources, the lakeshore Métis retained only a nominal knowledge of (and identification with) their French-Canadian forefathers' Catholicism.[63] Yet, they were desirous to see their children (both from their Métis and Indian wives) learn new ways:

> J'ai trouvé à la Baie des Canards tous les Métis et sauvages qui ont coutumes d'hiverner et quelques autres qui passent ordinairement l'hiver sur la montagne… Tout le monde à la Baie des Canards s'est approché des sacrements exceptés les scandaleux que vous connaissez et qui font mon désespoir. Chose étrange, ils sont les plus désireux à faire instruire leurs enfants!

> *At Duck Bay, I found all the Métis and Indians who habitually winter there along with a few others who usually winter on the mountain… Everybody in Duck Bay partook in the holy sacraments except for the scandalous few that are my despair. Strangely, they are the most desirous of seeing their children receive (religious) instructions.*[64]

Having some contact with the Red River Settlement and the HBC through their trading activities and prior living arrangements, it is possible that the lakeshore trading Métis were aware of the drastic changes looming on the horizon. For example, members of the Chartrand clan made a point of maintaining friendly relations with the priest whatever the nature of their marital activities in the northern part of the lake. During the 1868 famine, Paulet and Antoine Chartrand sold a thousand white fish to Mgr. Taché when they could probably have received a better price from other elements of the Red River Settlement population.[65]

Two other families were settling in the area by the late 1850s and early 1860s. The first is the extended family of John Monkman.[66] He was the son of a well-to-do trader, James Monkman, who had retired at Red River with his wife, Marie Cree. John Monkman was married to Mary Josèphte Richard. She was the daughter of the Saulteaux village residents François Richard and Marguerite Sauteuse. The Monkmans were heavily involved in the manufacture of salt on Lake Winnipegosis. They had close ties with the HBC, and during *les evénements* at least one member of the family actively supported the Canadian Party and tried to instigate "Indians" to revolt against what Riel called the "old settlements," i.e., the Métis communities.[67] This may have been due in part to desperation: during the 1868 famine, "widow" Mary Monkman with four dependents was listed as being indigent.

The second extended family, the Delarondes, is also an intriguing case. Louis Delaronde Sr. worked as a clerk for the HBC from 1815 (Athabasca expedition) to the merger of 1821 (Peace River Post), when he became a freeman at Red River. He married Madeleine Boucher, who was also the daughter of fairly active free traders. Like the Chartrands, the Delarondes were involved in freighting and trading with the Native population after 1821. The scale of their operations was impressive: in their winter camps they employed several hired hands (as opposed to family members). Also, unlike the four "old" families, they appear to have maintained ties with the HBC. In February 1868 Father Simonet visited their winter camp:

> Le 27 je suis parti de la Baie des Canards en compagnie de quatre traiteurs qui eurent la complaisance de me prêter deux chiens pour remplacer ceux des miens qui étaient hors de service... Nous arrivâmes la même journée à la Rivière Poule d'Eau chez les Laronde qui me reçurent avec leur bienveillance ordinaire. Les Catholiques engagés à ces messieurs et à la Compagnie vinrent se confesser dans la soirée. Le lendemain Etienne Laronde [Delaronde] eut la charité de me mener jusqu'à la Rivière aux Grues en allant voir les sauvages.[68]

> *On the 27th I left Duck Bay in the company of four traders who were kind enough to lend me two dogs to replace my own which was out of commission... We stopped the same day at Water Hen River at the Larondes who received me with their usual kindness. The Catholics in the employ of the Larondes, along with those working for the Company, came to confession that evening. The following day, Etienne Laronde [Delaronde] was kind enough to take me as far as Crane River on his way to seeing the Indians.*

Louis Delaronde was a French Canadian married to a Métisse, Madeleine Boucher. All their children listed in the 1870 Saint-Laurent census were born in the Red River Settlement. Comments in the Oblate correspondence give the impression that the children had received varying amounts of education at Saint-Boniface Catholic schools. Though actively engaged in trading, their ties to the local Saulteaux population were not as direct as those of the four founding families. None appear to have cohabited with or married "Native" women, and missionaries make no mention of "improper" behaviour in their winter camps prior to 1870. Their daily spoken language was French *mitchif* as opposed to the Cree dialect used by the other families. Interestingly, the Delarondes' relations to the Chartrand extended family seem to have been uneasy. They were allied with the Monkman family when it came to the tension with the Chartrands. This tension predated the 1861 death of John Monkman, who was killed by Paulet Chartrand during a drunken dispute.[69] This tension could have stemmed partly from a growing competition over a slowly shrinking trading and freighting market. The children of Louis Delaronde Sr. would not marry into any of the families originating from the Saulteaux village. It is only in the third generation, after 1870, that traditional Fond du Lac or Baie St-Paul spousal names emerge.

The origins, composition and behaviour of the Delarondes are indicative of some of the families that would be heading north in the difficult decade of 1865–75. The Boyer, Daigneault, and Goulet families coming up from the Red River were (or had been) more settled, endogamous (in the sense of not marrying into the fur-trapping "Indian" segment of the population), more religiously docile and, with the decline of the bison hunt, more interested in agriculture.[70] They appear not to have had the freighting and trading skills of the earlier families and consequently had little to fall back on when the 1868 famine hit. Several of their names appear on the indigent list prepared by the local Saint-Laurent priest, Father Camper. Families that were moving northward to the Saint-Laurent area in the 1860s and 1870s were interested in commercial fishing combined with some gardening and cattle raising (and bison hunting as long as it lasted). Their economic activities linked more closely to the southern part of the lake and they never established the close ties with the "Indian" fur trappers[71] enjoyed by the families originating from the Saulteaux village and on the shores of Lake Manitoba.[72]

The essential differences between the Freemen, the traders and the Métis from the southern parishes were not "biological"; they were not simply questions of race. Most of these people had both Native and *voyageur* (or Orkneyman) ancestors. What distinguished and fragmented this population were different economic activities and places of residence in the first half of the 19th century, their adaptations and responses to changing circumstances after 1850, and their relations with church and company authorities. For example, the trading and fishing segments led different lifestyles. Distinctions were also imposed from above, as illustrated by the already mentioned incident involving Chartrand and his Protestant friends. Oblate missionaries, imbued with a western European racist ideology, perpetuated a process of racialisation by emphasising further distinctions along religious and linguistic lines and interpreting them in racial terms. Missionary letters are filled with such interpretations. During the worst of the famine of 1867–68,[73] the local Oblate, Father Simonet, apparently unaware of the effects of starvation, explained the "Métis" lack of interest in doing *corvée* work for the mission as resulting from their inherently "indolent" character and their laziness.[74] These views permeated the francophone religious orders well into the 20th century. The resident priest for the parish of Sainte-Claire,[75] assessing the economic prospects of his parish, argued that even though the local "Métis" were reasonably well off,

> Quant aux Métis qui composent en grande partie ma paroisse, à part de respectable exceptions, ils sont une bande de dégénérés, de jouisseurs... La chose capitale pour l'avenir de Sainte-Claire est de remplacer en grande partie les Métis par des familles Canadiennes-françaises, autrement nous aurons le même résultat qu'à Saint-Laurent.[76]

As for the Métis who make up the majority in my parish, apart from a few respectable exceptions, they are a bunch of degenerate pleasure seekers... The key thing for Sainte-Claire is to replace the greater number of the Métis by French Canadian families, otherwise we will have the same result as in Saint-Laurent.

In other words, in the eyes of the clergy, poverty, marginalisation and even cultural traditions were the result of an unchangeable, biologically inherited predisposition. The plight of the Métis was not even partly the result of a shrinking fur-trade staple-producing economy, difficult agrarian conditions, and receding bison herds.

Whatever the merits of the ecclesiastical assessment of "Métis" character, the hunting and fishing Métis were experiencing severe stress and dislocation in the 1860s and 1870s because of the decline of the fur trade centred on Red River, coupled with the decimation of the bison herds. The devastating famine of 1868 that saw the combined failure of the bison hunt, the fishing industry, and farming, followed by the transfer of power from the HBC to the Canadian government in 1870, would have long-term adverse effects on Saint-Laurent's poorer families.[77]

CHAPTER 2

Adapting to a New Order, 1850–1871

THE OAK POINT AND SAINT-LAURENT AREA DID NOT present a very encouraging view for outsiders passing through at the beginning of the famine in the summer of 1867. The "run-down" collection of tents and houses[1] set up in a haphazard fashion inspired little confidence. There were no real roads, no fences, and few gardens; in short, very little of the things commonly associated with small peasant settlements found in rural Canada or Europe. In fact, Donald Gunn, passing through on an egging expedition in 1867, did not even recognise these people as being of the same stock as the Red River Settlement Métis:

> In this region there are at present three small villages; one at Oak Point, containing 10 to 15 dwellings, called houses of the most primitive kind; another at what is called the Bay [Saint-Laurent] consisting of seven or eight houses, and favored as the residence of the Catholic priest. A third village is rising two or three miles to the south of the latter [Isle de Pierre—the future Saint-Ambroise]. The population of these villages is composed of Indians, of half, three-quarter, and of seven–eight Indians, with a very few aged French-Canadians.[2]

Because of their dwellings, general aspects, and apparent lifestyle, Gunn labelled the inhabitants he saw as "Indians" but, as is obvious from his description of their seasonal activities, he was seeing only one segment of the local population. The primary reason for his disapproval was that these people did not farm.[3] The poor soil, the distance from market, repeated crop failures and, most important, the existence of viable lucrative alternatives tied to the fur-trade economy did not count in his equation:

> These people are like the fowl of heaven; they neither sow nor reap, nor do they even as far as I have been able to see, plant potatoes. They possess a few cattle and horses; the latter roam through the wood summer and winter, living independent of their masters' care. The finest hay grows within a few yards of their houses, yet I have been informed that many of these people are so indolent as to allow their animals to die in winter from starvation. There are two or three exceptions to the above rule.[4]

Gunn goes on to describe the seasonal activities of the lakeshore inhabitants. In early spring they would catch fish that swarmed into the many little creeks flowing into the lake from the east. By May these easily-caught fish would have returned to the lake, and the "Indians," as he calls them, would shoot ducks and geese (just returning from migration to the south) until the birds left the area in late May. Thereafter, their main food source would be muskrats and birds' eggs until July. Then the lakeshore dwellers would find subsistence very difficult, "unless possessed of a means to enable them to draw on the settlement for flour" (such as the exchange of pelts, salt, smoked/dried fish). In October the whitefish came near the shore for spawning, "and those who command a little industry *and plenty of nets* will be able to lay in a good stock for winter use."[5]

Interestingly, Gunn is only describing food-gathering activities carried out by men (except perhaps the egg collecting). This "man the hunter" stereotype would be common amongst anthropologists of the first half of the 20th century. Surely Métis women were also active in the search for food. Their descendants, as was discovered in the course of interviewing, are still knowledgeable about edible berries, roots, and mushrooms.

In fact, according to Gunn, these Métis women could willingly and expertly step into what would be considered a man's role by 19th-century Europeans. In one specific case Gunn talks of a woman coming back from commercial dealings in the Settlement:

> Here we overtook our companions of last night, and a heroic dame from Oak Point, who left her home a few days before for Red River, and was now on her way back with two cart loads of pine boards and planks. She has a considerable portion of white blood, yet exhibits all the hardiness of the squaw, and can, with wonderful dexterity, avail herself of all the resources of the forest and the lake.[6]

The earlier qualification, "plenty of nets," is also interesting. Materials for nets had to be bought and represented a capital outlay. Not all the "Métis" would have been in a position (in this of all years) to come up with the necessary cash or items of trade.

The people described by the egg collector were obviously from the non-trading and salt-making segment of the Lake Manitoba population (minus the "two or three exceptions"), and were enduring an unusually difficult year. Gunn makes no mention of bison-hunting activities that remained important up to the early 1870s, except for the disastrous years of 1867 and 1868. Also, he makes no mention of winter ice fishing that some people at wintering camps were still pursuing on a commercial scale during those difficult years.[7] Finally, he does not mention the traders and their followers present mostly at Oak Point but also at Saint-Laurent until at least 1872[8] and whom the 1868 Relief Committee did not consider indigent.

Gunn may be describing two groups of people. First, the displaced, impoverished Métis from Saint-François Xavier and the Red River parishes who were retreating to the lakeshore in the hopes of finding a livelihood in fishing. Second, the elusive Freeman Métis who usually just passed through Saint-Laurent and Oak Point on the way to trading their furs at the Forks (and to the bison hunt) in spring and on their return trips to their wintering camps in autumn. With the complete failure of the fishing season, added to the crop failure and poor returns in the bison hunts, Métis coming up from the southern parishes may well have been living an uncharacteristically hand-to-mouth existence in 1867 and 1868. The others, Freemen Métis, led a life similar to that of the Saulteaux trapping segment and perhaps, to an outsider, would have appeared as one and the same.[9] The fact that a longtime resident of the Red River Settlement, with a Métis wife, would label both these groups of Métis as "Indian" points once again to these people's fluid socioeconomic position, especially in times of stress.[10]

NORMALISE	PRENOMS	M	F	M12	TOTAL	HO	OX	CO	CA	BUSO	W67	P67	W68	P68	PARISH		NOTES
BONNEAU	FRANCOIS	1	2	0	3	0	0	1	2	0	0	0	0	0	ST-LAURENT	I	INDIGENT
BOYER	PIERRE	5	3	3	8	1	0	0	0	10	0	25	0	0	ST-LAURENT	I	INDIGENT
CHABOYER	ANTOINE	1	1	0	2	1	0	1	1	0	0	0	0	0	ST-LAURENT		
CHABOYER	CHARLES	3	4	5	7	0	0	0	0	0	0	0	0	0	ST-LAURENT		INDIGENT
CHABOYER	JOSEPH	2	3	3	5	2	0	0	0	0	0	0	0	0	ST-LAURENT		
CHABOYER	NORBERT	1	2	1	3	2	0	1	1	0	0	0	0	0	ST-LAURENT		
CHABOYER	PIERRE	2	2	2	4	3	2	3	4	0	0	0	0	0	ST-LAURENT		
CHABOYER	VEUVE	3	1	1	4	1	0	1	1	4	0	0	0	0	ST-LAURENT	I	INDIGENT
CHARTRAND	ANTOINE	3	4	4	7	0	1	0	1	5	0	20	0	0	ST-LAURENT		
CHARTRAND	PAUL (FILS)	3	3	4	6	0	1	1	2	4	0	30	0	0	ST-LAURENT		
CHARTRAND	PAULET	3	1	1	4	0	2	1	1	10	0	60	0	10	ST-LAURENT		
DAGNON	RAINAULD	2	2	2	4	1	0	0	0	5	0	0	0	0	ST-LAURENT	I	INDIGENTS
DELARONDE	ETIENNE	3	3	4	6	2	0	2	2	0	0	0	0	0	ST-LAURENT		
DELARONDE	LOUISON	6	3	3	9	10	3	3	2	0	0	0	0	0	ST-LAURENT		
DEMONTIGNY	CHARLES	3	3	1	6	3	0	0	0	0	0	0	0	0	ST-LAURENT		
DEMONTIGNY	CHARLES (FILS)	1	1	0	2	2	0	0	0	0	0	0	0	0	ST-LAURENT		
DESJARLAIS	JOSEPH	1	1	0	2	1	0	0	0	0	0	0	0	0	ST-LAURENT	I	INDIGENTS
DESJARLAIS	JOSEPHTE	2	3	0	5	1	0	1	1	3	0	0	0	0	ST-LAURENT		
DESJARLAIS	MICHEL	3	3	2	6	3	0	0	0	0	0	0	0	0	ST-LAURENT	I	INDIGENT
DUCHARME	BAPTISTE	5	6	4	11	2	0	0	0	0	0	0	0	0	ST-LAURENT	I	INDIGENT
DUCHARME	LOUISON	4	3	2	7	0	0	1	1	0	0	0	0	0	ST-LAURENT	I	INDIGENT
GOULET	PIERRE	2	2	2	4	2	1	1	2	4	0	10	0	0	ST-LAURENT		
LAVALLEE	ANDRE	2	1	1	3	1	0	1	1	0	0	0	0	0	ST-LAURENT		
LAVALLEE	ANTOINE	2	1	1	3	2	0	0	0	0	0	0	0	0	ST-LAURENT		
LAVALLEE	BAPTISTE	2	2	0	4	0	1	1	1	5	0	35	0	10	ST-LAURENT		
LAVALLEE	BAPTISTE (FILS)	2	3	2	5	3	1	2	2	3	0	0	0	2	ST-LAURENT		
LAVALLEE	JOSEPH	4	3	5	7	3	1	2	3	4	0	40	0	0	ST-LAURENT		
MCLEOD	ABRAHAM	4	2	3	6	4	1	3	4	5	0	25	0	1	ST-LAURENT		
MCLEOD	JOSEPHTE (VEUVE)	1	3	2	4	0	0	2	1	0	0	0	0	0	ST-LAURENT	I	INDIGENTS
MONKMAN	MARY (VEUVE JOHNY)	1	4	2	5	3	0	0	0	4	0	9	0	0	ST-LAURENT	I	INDIGENTS
PANGMAN	PIERRE	3	4	2	7	0	0	1	1	0	0	0	0	0	ST-LAURENT	I	INDIGENT
PAUL	ST MATH	4	4	2	8	2	0	0	0	0	0	0	0	0	ST-LAURENT	I	INDIGENT
RICHARD	FRANCOIS	2	1	0	3	0	0	1	1	2	0	10	0	0	ST-LAURENT	I	INDIGENTS
RICHARD	FRANCOIS	6	3	2	9	0	0	0	0	0	0	20	0	2	ST-LAURENT	-I	INDIGENT
RICHARD	PIERRE	6	4	5	10	0	1	1	2	5	0	0	0	0	ST-LAURENT	I	INDIGENT
WABIKEG	PIERRE	2	3	2	5	0	0	0	0	0	0	0	0	0	ST-LAURENT	I	INDIGENTS

1868 Census entries : M = male; F = Female; MI = Minor (under 12 years of age); TO = Total; HO = Horses; OX = Oxen; CO = Cows; CA = Calves; BUS = Bushels usually sown [unspec ified]; W67 = wheat crop in 1867 [bushels]; P68 = potato crop in 1867 [bushels]; W67 = wheat crop in 1868 [bushels]; P68 = potato crop in 1868 [bushels]; Parish -I = indigent

The impact of the famine was not uniform throughout the Saint-Laurent-Oak Point population. As mentioned above, many of those who were listed as non-indigent were from the trading and salt-making segment.[11] The statistical summary produced by the Executive Relief Committee indicates that 17 out of 36 households (47%) were in need of immediate relief (see Relief Committee Census Returns, above). Several names from the founding families are missing, perhaps indicating that many households were trying their luck in other parts of the lake. Also, many of the less prominent (and more transient) Lake Manitoba Métis who traditionally wintered at Duck Bay counted on fishing and bison hunting to feed their families and produce an exchangeable commodity. They could not afford to spend a season in an area where returns were so disappointing. Furthermore, these lakeshore Métis, unlike perhaps Métis of the more settled parishes, would have known of other areas of the lakes where fish catches might be more plentiful.

For many Métis arriving from the southern settlements, Saint-Laurent and Oak Point seem to have been the farthest north they were willing to go. Unfortunately, they did not find much relief:

> Outre mes gens, ceux de la Rivière Rouge et surtout ceux de la Prairie de Cheval Blanc sont venus tous les jours me demander quelque service. Et aujourd'hui j'ai la douleur de les renvoyer sans autre soulagement que des paroles de compassion. Or l'hiver n'est pas encore commencé. La pêche, qui a commencé plus tôt que de coutume et avec une bonne apparence de réussite, est à peu près nulle pour une bonne partie, bien médiocre pour la plupart.[12]

> *Besides my own people, those of Red River and especially those of the White Horse Prairie come every day to ask me for some help. And today, to my distress, I was forced to send them away without tangible help but only words of compassion. And winter has not yet started. Fishing, which began earlier than usual and with some promise of success, is now largely mediocre.*

The southern migrants were also faced with another locust devastation in Saint-Laurent and "not a vegetable was to be had in the mission." According to information gleaned from the missionary correspondence, these new residents joined with their neighbours in pursuing non-farming, staple-producing activities:

> Bien des gens de la Prairie du Cheval Blanc [Saint-François Xavier] viennent s'établir ici... Ici comme à la Rivière Rouge les sauterelles mangent tout. Le poisson est notre seule ressource.[13]

> *Many people from the White Horse Prairie [Saint-François Xavier] come here to settle... Here, like in Red River, the grasshoppers eat everything. Fishing is our only resource.*

Perhaps because of the arrival of economic refugees to the area, Saint-Laurent was the parish with the highest proportion of indigents. Of the 36 families listed, fully 17 (47%) were labelled "indigent." Interestingly, the parish with the next highest rate of destitute families was Baie Saint-Paul with 14 of 64 (21.8%) families in need. In the larger and older settlement of Saint-François Xavier, only 14 families out of 166 surveyed (8.4%) required immediate assistance. It would seem those most in need congregated along the shores, in an area they were familiar with, hoping to subsist on the fisheries.

Interestingly, as southern Métis (former full-time bison hunters and farmers) were moving towards the Saint-Laurent mission, many of the old Lake Manitoba settlers were leaving. In previous years, some traders following the retreating "fur" frontier had established themselves in Duck Bay. In 1868–69 Métis fishermen looking for more plentiful fish stocks joined the traders. Fishing in the northern part of Lake Manitoba and in Lake Winnipegosis does not appear to have failed as greatly as in the Saint-Laurent-Oak Point area[14]:

> Dans les circonstances actuelles, la population de la Baie des Canards ne peut que s'accroître. Déjà elle s'accroît. Quelques [nouvelles] familles veulent s'y établir. Un plus grand nombre y auraient hiverné, s'ils avaient trouvé de la place dans les barges. Je connais plusieurs personnes qui iraient à la Baie des Canards s'il y avait un prêtre résident.[15]

> *Given the current situation, the Duck Bay population can only increase. Already it is growing. Some [new] families wish to settle here. An even greater number had wanted to winter here but found no places on the barges. I know several persons who would go to Duck Bay if a priest was in residence there.*

The years 1869–70 were no better for the southern part of the lake. The chronicles note that in 1869 the grasshoppers came again to Saint-Laurent and Oak Point. The *Codex Historicus* states that "black" flour was selling for $7 for a 100-pound bag, "sometimes $10.00," obviously considered an exorbitant price by the author. It is therefore not surprising that the starving segment of the population took action:

> In March 1870 during the Riel Rebellion the Half-Breeds took possession of the H.B.Co. Post at Oak Point and killed some eight to ten head of cattle, distributed the beef among themselves as well as some dry goods taken from the store. Mr. Deschambault* who was then in charge made no resistance but handed over the keys and he then left and took up lodging in a neighbouring house. The Half-Breeds treated him very kindly and furnished him with fresh meat and other necessaries.[16]

Father Camper, returning from mission work on March 17, was not pleased with the seizure and wrote to Louis Riel for instructions. Riel, apparently much dismayed, ordered the return of the store and goods to the man in charge:

> Nos gens se sont conformés immédiatement et sans réplique aux ordres de Monsieur le Président; la force d'un gouvernement pour bien des gens a souvent plus d'efficacité que la voix de la conscience.[17]

> *Our people obeyed immediately, without arguments, to the President's orders. The voice of a government seems to resonate more strongly with many people than the voice of a conscience!*

The people involved in the seizure were not the Lake Manitoba traders or the

---

* Probably the son of French-Canadian Île-à-la-Crosse postmaster G. Deschambault and his "Métis" wife Isabelle Hamelin.

Métis salt-fish-pelt commodity producers[18] who were still wintering on Lake Winnipegosis in March. They would not have arrived at *La Mission* till the end of May.[19] Those implicated were the Métis who had been coming up from the more southerly settlements to flee the famine. The crops had failed once more the previous summer, fishing had been poor in the autumn and spring[20] and the fact that they took cattle would indicate the bison hunt had failed. That they were from the Red River area would explain the speed of their obedience to Riel's orders. He was a familiar figure to them and his family was well respected. Nothing was found in the historical documents to indicate the "old" lakeshore families were actively sympathetic to his cause.

Things would not improve for the "new" settlers from the southern parishes. In fact, the seizure brought only fleeting relief for the desperate families. Commenting on the months following the March takeover, Brother Mulvihill, OMI, states:

> After March [came a] time of hunger. There was no flour to be found just dried jackfish. A métis, François Bonneau* was suffering from extreme want and poverty. He once had been a buffalo hunter. [Bonneau tells the chronicler] "I have eaten nothing in the last 3 days save and except 'des petites poires qui me donnent la chiche, mon corps est toujours lâche et je suis bien faible'." Bonneau had been one of the bravest [hunters] on the plain.[21]

Nevertheless, many of the displaced Métis families remained in the Saint-Laurent area. They gave up their bison-hunting activities and switched over to commercial fishing even though it would be an unprofitable enterprise in the southern end of the lake for at least one more season.[22] It would be years before any serious attempts at commercial farming would again be tried.[23] Yet these southern Métis and the Freemen and trading Métis hedged their bets, putting up fences and attempting to plant some sort of garden in the summer of 1871 as they waited for the land surveyors to come:

> Les gens se remuent en plein pour semer. Plusieurs charroyent des perches en masse. *Je ne doute pas que ce soit la Montagne qui enfante une souris*; cependant il y en a quelques uns qui sèmeront certainement dix, quinze et même vingt barils de patates, c'est toujours un commencement.[24]

---

* François Bonneau was a Roman Catholic Métis born in 1794. The Bonneau family, according to the censuses, appears to have resided largely in the Saint-François Xavier and Baie St-Paul areas. His wife was Marie Favel (b. 1795), the daughter of Humphrey Favel (son of a senior HBC official) and Jenny, an Indian woman. François Bonneau is listed as residing in Grantown in 1843 and owning a house, a stable, three horses, two mares, a calf, a pig, two oxen, two cows, four carts, and working one acre. The number of carts indicates that Bonneau was actively engaged in the pemmican and robe industry on quite a large scale. By the 1868 census he was listed as an "indigent."

> *The people are bestirring themselves for seeding. Many are transporting great quantities of posts. I have no doubt it is a mountain birthing a mouse; however a few will sow 10, 15 or even 20 barrels of potatoes, and it is a beginning.*

The derogatory comment is not surprising, coming as it does from a missionary with a farming background looking at the activities of "half-breeds," most of whom had never farmed on any scale. Also, as usual, farming would conflict with other more lucrative business such as fishing: "Les gens ne paraissent pas très enthousiasmés pour faire un grand effort d'agriculture, la pêche a bonne apparence, voilà le point de mir [*sic*] de toutes leurs pensées."[25] "*The people are not enthusiastic about working the land. The fisheries are promising and are the focus of everyone's thoughts.*" Yet several Métis had a good idea of the potential value of land. Some were marking out claims in February of 1872,[26] of which the government surveyor, William Wagner, arriving at the lakeshore in the spring of 1872 took no account.[27]

By the early 1870s, the Métis of Saint-Laurent and Oak Point had experienced years of economic difficulty and social upheaval. These were the results of natural calamities affecting an embryonic agriculture, an economy in transition (saturation of the pemmican trade, receding bison herds, and the western attraction of the robe trade), and political turmoil. In the spring of 1872 the Métis were faced with the further challenge of securing claim to lands they occupied. Not all the inhabitants of the Saint-Laurent area fared equally well in this legal process. Occupations they engaged in and lifestyles they led in the years leading up to the survey would influence the outcome. As will be documented, Métis traders, hunter-fishermen and farmer-fishermen differed in their ability, and their willingness, to meet the demands made by the Dominion Lands Branch.

Initially the population of Lake Manitoba attempted to claim a large tract of land collectively, to be set aside as a Métis reserve, including river lots and land situated behind the lots. All the Métis parishes claimed tracts of land in 1870–71 by publishing a statement of occupation and a description of the claim in the local paper, *Le Métis*.[28] The first attempt to secure land in Saint-Laurent was made under the leadership of Louis Delaronde of the Saint-Boniface trading family. In the following year, 1872, the surveyor William Wagner came up to the lake to delineate the river lots and register land claims. After 1872, efforts to secure letters patent seem to have been made on an individual rather than a collective basis.

William Wagner, of the Dominion Lands Branch, surveyed the settlement of Oak Point between April 29 and May 6, 1872. He then moved down to Saint-Laurent and worked there between May 7 and May 13. He was unimpressed with the inhabitants of both settlements and scoffed at some of their land claims. At Oak Point he described the inhabitants as "mostly either traders (furs, etc.) or their followers and fishermen." He noted that with the exception of a few fenced-in patches of land on which potatoes and like vegetables were growing, no agricultural business had been carried out. He did add that the land was mostly covered with scrubby oak and a few poplars "and with exception of interspersing meadows or hay ground very stony and gravelly and therefore holds out little inducement for farming."[29]

Wagner thought that the claims put forth by the Saint-Laurent and Oak Point Métis (who had forced him to hire a local interpreter who could speak both English and their "Indian brogue") were "somewhat extravagant." But his assessment was based on the little use they seemed to have for their land and their general lifestyle, *not* because of their "mixed" background. Although he was amused by their use of the term "white" to define themselves, he was also quite concerned because, during the survey and for some time prior, the Métis had been trying to persuade those they considered to be "Indian" to leave the area:

> It appears to me as where all Halfbreeds up here are of the opinion that a full-bred Indian had no right to hold any property amongst *whites*, if I may call the settlers at Oak Point by that name... but where this presumption is erroneous I beg to draw your attention to the two Indians [having] houses [in the settlement]. There are other houses owned by Indians close to the road and southerly to the former. It is true the houses are unoccupied at present but I fear that their neighbours have impressed on these poor men the idea that they could not hold property. I should not have dwelt upon their subject to such an extent had I not seen during the last winter that Indians settled outside the reserves were told to leave and build upon the reserve.[30]

Such an attitude is doubly surprising when we consider the individuals involved. Several of the Chartrand clan were implicated in the affair even though, for example, Paulet Chartrand's mother had been labelled "Indian" by religious authorities and his son, Antoine, actually had an official Indian wife living with him at the time of the 1870 census. Most, if not all, of the Saint-Laurent and Oak Point residents had mothers, wives, mothers-in-law or grandmothers who were or had been labelled "Indian" by HBC or ecclesiastical authorities or by the 1870 census takers. The fact of their own partially Native ancestry did nothing to soften the attitudes of the inhabitants of Saint-Laurent.

Several explanations come to mind. It is possible that the old Lake Manitoba Métis residents, with close ties to the Saulteaux populations, were reacting to the opinions of the recently arrived Saint-François Xavier and Red River Settlement Métis, who had not in the recent past been closely allied to "Indians." Or, perhaps, the old Freemen and trading Lake Manitoba Métis families were perpetuating the distinction between themselves and the Saulteaux of Lake Winnipegosis. Trading and even marital alliances were somehow distinct from general cohabitation. Finally, it is possible that the Métis saw the land claims as a manner of creating a Métis reserve. They would be using their own definition of "Métis"—perhaps, "Cree-speaker from elsewhere"—since for many non-trading lakeshore Métis in the 1860s and 1870s their lifestyle was by and large indistinguishable from that of the Saulteaux Indians. The problem is that we do not know if all segments of the Métis population approved of the "Indian" displacement or if the trading or Red River families mainly instigated it. From the Saint-Laurent and Oak Point reserve all those perceived to be non-Métis were to be excluded.[31]

However, the argument that the Saint-Laurent area Métis wished to create an all-Métis reserve, as opposed to simply excluding those considered Indians, is not very convincing. They were letting a Scotsman, Alexander Begg, make a land claim on Lot 2 of Oak Point. Another possible explanation for the apparent antipathy towards the local Saulteaux residents may have been simple jealousy. These "Indians" were not necessarily the impoverished fringe dwellers in the lakeshore settlements. Gunn would encounter an "Indian" family from Oak Point during his 1867 egging expedition:

> While here [Shoal Lake] we were joined by an Indian, his squaw and their son. These people had been to the settlement with their spring trade. They had two carts and were taking back in exchange for their furs, flour, clothing, and ammunition. This Indian resides in a house in Oak Point, and is reputed the best hunter in the district, which fact accounts satisfactorily for his comparative wealth.[32]

As stated earlier, the difficulty with Gunn's assessment is his tendency to designate Métis as "half ... seven-eight *Indians*." We cannot be sure if he is discussing a Métis or a Saulteaux hunter. All that can be ascertained is that the number of people regarded as "Indian" by both the civil and religious authorities abruptly diminished in the following decade. Wagner's opinion of the Saint-Laurent "French Halfbreeds" is not much more favourable. There may have been ulterior motives to Wagner's low opinion of the Métis:

> Monsieur l'arpenteur Wagner veut définitivement s'établir au lac, ou au moins y passer l'hiver avec toute sa famille [...] Si je me trompe l'idée serait d'éloigner les métis bien loin, et y attirer des étrangers. La place a l'air de lui plaire beaucoup.[33]

> *The surveyor, Mr. Wagner, definitely wants to settle by the lake. Or, at the very least, spend the winter there with all his family. I may be wrong but his idea would be to disperse the Metis so as to attract strangers. I think he really likes the place.*

As mentioned above, he surveyed the land in early May prior to the general arrival of the traders and northern *hivernants*.[34] There were only 25 settlers residing at the mission whom Wagner describes as hunters or fishermen.[35] He noted only a few potato patches in the settlement and criticised the Métis settlers for not being agriculturally active:

> With the exception of a few potato patches nothing showed to signs of agriculture although the ground is well adapted for the culture of all cereals... I allude to it only for the purpose of showing the Dept what use of land is made here, and yet every one of these people expecting to have four miles back from the Lake.[36]

Neither was Wagner very sympathetic to the trading and commodity-producing families who had to regularly displace themselves to the northern lakes. Even *notables* like Michel Chartrand were not well regarded. The surveyor noted that the claimant to Lot 1, Michel Chartrand, only had an old house (no improvement) on his land and, being a trader at Dog Lake and Waterhen River, he only came down "on visits" during the summer season. Obviously, from the tone of the report, Wagner did not feel an old house and yearly visits entitled Chartrand to a land grant.

According to the 1870 census[37] there were 41 heads of family living in the Saint-Laurent and Oak Point area.[38] The total population at the time of the survey, counting women, children and adult dependents, was approximately 300 people. Of these, 24 heads of family, having 14 different surnames, were "Lakeshore" or "northern Métis." They came from outside the Red River area.[39] These surnames include the four founding clans (see 1870 Manitoba Census chart, next page) and 10 other families that had been dwelling at least part of the year in Saint-Laurent since the early 1860s. The 10 "Freemen" families may have been present prior to 1860, but lack of archival evidence makes their presence impossible to detect. Two of the Freemen families, the Missiapits and the Aignases, were listed as being of "Indian" descent in the census. Another 17 Métis heads of family, having 10 different surnames, declared their place of birth to be the Red River Settlement or White Horse Plains. At least five of the southern families had been in the Saint-Laurent area since the 1867–68 famine years.

In the spring of 1872, Wagner surveyed a total of 40 river lots in the Saint-Laurent and Oak Point area. He registered 26 claims made by resident Métis heads of household. It is interesting to note who was present that spring to make land claims. Two of the area's founding families, the Pangmans and the Sayers, possibly the earliest families to settle there, were completely unrepresented. The Lavallées claimed only three river lots in the mission area. The Chartrand family, with key members missing, made at most only four claims in the Saint-Laurent-Oak Point area. It should be noted that four related Chartrand families were living on a single river lot in Oak Point. They had erected houses and stables on the lot, and some of the members were obviously residing in Oak Point year round, but they did not seem to see the land in terms of its potential for farm use. Except for the Lavallées, these early families do not appear eager to secure large tracts of land. They needed a *pied-à-terre* for their summer activities and not much more. Pierre Chartrand, for example, ran a store on his lot (Lot 2 in Saint-Laurent) and did not engage in any farming activities. Four Freemen Lake Manitoba families are listed as laying claims to river lots. The Ducharmes[40] (originally from Pembina) claimed two lots, the Desjarlais[41] claimed one, and the Richards[42] (children of HBC interpreter and long-time resident of the lake, François Richard) claimed one. Abraham McLeod[43] of Duck River claimed one lot in Oak Point. Finally, the largest family block of claims was made by the Chaboyers[44] who claimed six river lots. The fact that they were present in early spring indicates that they were active in commercial fishing at the south end of the lake rather than trading up north. The Chaboyers obviously had some appreciation of the potential value of land.

Southern Métis families originating from Saint-François Xavier and the Red River Settlement occupied the remainder of the lots claimed. Several other lots

1870 Manitoba Census

Oak Point

Heads of Household	Age	Where Born	People in Household	School age Children
CHARTRAND				
PAUL (I)	58	**Duck River**	5	3
Paul (II)	32	Lac Manitoba	8	3
Louis (II)	30	Duck River	7	3
Antoine (II)	36	Lac Manitoba	9	5
Baptiste (II)	26	White Horse Plains	4	0
Totals			**33**	**14**
SAYER				
JOHN	30	**Rivière du Cygne**	5	0
BAPTISTE	70	**Ile-à-la-Crosse**	2	0
Totals			**7**	**0**
LAVALLÉE				
BAPTISTE	70	**Ile-à-la-Crosse**	4	1
André (I)	28	Lac Manitoba	4	0
Joseph (I)	36	Lac Manitoba	8	4
Baptiste (I)	29	Lac Manitoba	5	1
Antoine (I)	26	Lac Manitoba	4	1
Totals			**25**	**7**

Lac Manitoba

Heads of Household	Age	Where Born	People in Household	School age Children
PANGMAN				
PIERRE	50	**Pembina**	9	4
unknown		Lac Manitoba	8	0
Totals			**17**	**4**
CHARTRAND				
PIERRE (I)	40	**Red River**	6	2
MICHEL (I)	41	**Lac Manitoba**	7	2
Totals			**13**	**4**

were claimed by families who had come up during the hard years of the previous decade such as the claimants of Saint-Laurent Lots 17 and 24—Louis Carrière[45] of the Red River Settlement and Pierre Boyer[46] of White Horse Plains. The old Saint-Boniface family, the Delarondes,[47] would claim a total of four lots. On one of them, Oak Point Lot 19, Paul Delaronde was running a small store and saloon, much to the scandal of the Catholic Church in Manitoba.[48] By the 1874 resurvey they had only one lot in Oak Point (Lot 10) but were still retaining their two lots at the more southerly Saint-Laurent agglomeration. One Métis *notable* from Red River, James McKay, would make a claim on river Lot 2 in Oak Point and finally another (northern) Métis, William Rose, from Moose Factory, would claim Lot 4.

Not all of the claims would be successful and more than one Métis family would lose courage and sell, or be swindled of their claims, before the patent came through.[49] But already in the initial claim process a pattern was emerging. Only 12 surnames (extended families) are found amongst the claimants. The mix is interesting. As noted above, two families, claiming seven lots, are from the old Fond du Lac trading clans. Five other families, claiming 11 lots, have surnames found in the 1840s Red River censuses as belonging to Saulteaux village residents. Among these are the five Chaboyer brothers,[50] claiming six lots.[51] A further four relatively well-off Red River/Saint-Boniface families claimed seven lots. Thus, all levels of Red River society were represented, in varying degrees, in the initial Manitoba land claims process for the Saint-Laurent and Oak Point area.

Twenty-one households listed in the 1870 census do not even figure in the initial 1872 land claim survey. Saint-François Xavier families drifting back to their old abodes to the south after the famine years were over and the political turmoil had subsided could perhaps explain the absence of some of these families. However, based on a comparison of the 1870 Lake Manitoba census with Table 5 in Sprague and Frye, this does not appear to have been the case.[52] Few of these southern Métis households would lay claim to land elsewhere in the province. Three northern Métis heads of families—Louis Ducharme (Lot 7), Baptiste Lavallée (Lot 8), and Baptiste Ducharme (Lot 9)—contested the initial land survey and made land claims in Saint-Laurent. Louis Ducharme and Baptiste Lavallée were successful. The remainder of both the early lakeshore Métis and the Red River and Saint-François Xavier Métis listed as residing in the parish of Saint-Laurent in 1870 appear not to have made land claims anywhere in the province of Manitoba.

Yet, parish records continue to mention many of these non-claimant Métis in the years immediately following 1870. Probably, they simply built their homes or tented on relatives' property, Crown land or vacant land held by speculators in the Saint-Laurent and Oak Point area.[53] What is interesting is that by the 1880s family names of individuals who had been listed in the Saint-Laurent 1870 census were found on lists of people living in Duck Bay, Sandy Bay and ebb and flow areas. Some Métis, especially those men and women linked to the Freemen and trading families, were associating themselves more closely with the northern "Indian" population.[54]

As mentioned in the previous chapter, the timing of the 1872 survey (early spring) was crucial. For several of the families who spent their summers in the Oak

Point and Saint-Laurent area, the *hivernage* period of the year was simply not over. In the months of April and May they would still be in their northern encampments surrounded by ice and snow. Furthermore, the vast majority of these families would not have met the occupancy criteria established in the early 1870s in a series of amendments made to the Manitoba Act. Métis had to show improvements—house, stables, gardens. Many Lake Manitoba families, even if they considered the south shore their "home," would have spent their time there in a tent and their subsistence activities would have seriously constrained any attempt at farming. Even if they had spent their summers on a specific parcel of land for several years in a row they could not claim continuous occupancy and therefore proprietorship.

In fact, in the spring of 1872 there were more heads of household in Saint-Laurent *per se* than just the 18 who laid claim to parcels of land. Between May 7–13, Wagner counted 25 heads of families in Saint-Laurent. Therefore, at least seven non-*hivernant* families were simply not considered for a claim. Lack of interest on the part of some Métis to register a claim is one possible explanation. Another might be that some of these people were the "Freemen" Métis who had opted to winter in the south but who were nevertheless living a hunting and gathering life similar to that of the "Indian" segment of the lakeshore population. They were not in a position to lay claim to land in 1872 or again in 1874.

Another problem faced by the Saint-Laurent and Oak Point Métis in the spring of 1872 was their late start in house building. Many of the families, even the more affluent, appear to have switched from a tent to a house only after 1870. The lack of tangible improvements affected both the Freemen and the trading elite. William Wagner, the surveyor, notes in his survey book for Saint-Laurent:

> You will find 4 more settlers inscribed on the place. Abraham McLeod, Louis Chartrand, Antoine Chartrand, Baptiste Chartrand, who have only very lately begun their building and therefore will not come under the Manitoba Act.[55]

Nevertheless, of the 18 lots claimed by Métis heads of families in Saint-Laurent in 1872, 14 were at least partially patented to the original claimant. This is a much higher success rate than in the more southerly parishes. The land claim process in Oak Point seems to have taken a different turn. Few if any Métis ever came to own land in Oak Point. None of the original claimants owned land there by 1900. Oral histories confirm that many Oak Point families were living on Crown land until the 1950s. Though the possibility exists of some families having "passed," it would seem the Oak Point Métis (the land-owning ones in any case) were completely displaced by immigrants.

Landowners or not, a majority of the families listed in the 1870 census had representatives in the Saint-Laurent area who, between 1870 and 1881, were slowly giving up their bison-hunting and salt-making activities. They focussed their attention on commercial fishing coupled with dairy farming, trapping, wild produce harvesting, occasional winter freighting on the lakes and, after the turn of the century, farm labour. Dairy farming would become a viable alternative for some of the Saint-

Laurent families who had been successful in securing letters patent and who had managed somehow to secure sufficient capital, expertise, and markets to bring the land into production. Whatever their subsistence activities, the majority of pre-1870 families, whether northern trading and Freemen families or those having come from the southern parishes, continued to reside in the Saint-Laurent area. Other families, listed as Métis in 1870, continued to come and settle in the area, attracted by the fishing and good pastureland. The number of Saint-Laurent families increased by 81 between 1870 and 1893.[56]

The various segments of the Saint-Laurent population listed as Métis in 1870 did not all fare well in the decade following the creation of Manitoba. A primary source of information for the period 1870 to 1881, the *Oblate Chronicles*, exhibits a curiously contradictory way of thinking. It criticises some of the Métis families for their lack of responsibility toward land ownership while, in the next paragraph, acknowledging their severe, crippling poverty, which would greatly impede any attempt at improving their land and would make the selling of scrip or sections a frequent necessity. Commenting on the land speculators that were operating in the area, Brother Mulvihill states:

> Few if any of the Half-Breeds availed themselves of this good occasion to procure and secure additional property, no, but they sold their "scrip" to speculators and land grabbers for what ever they could get for it. This scrip was sold for 35 cents on the dollar... The Half-Breeds of this parish as well as other parishes not only sold their scrip but also the 240 acre lot which each obtained ... not one of them owns a 240 acre lot just now in 1895 at least in this parish.[57]

The scrip Father Mulvihill is alluding to was that given to Métis heads of family. The 240-acre lots refer to the allotments reserved for Métis who were minors in 1870. In the two parishes studied by this researcher (Sainte-Agathe and Saint-Laurent) no children ever actually came into possession of their 240 acres.

Despite chronic material difficulties a majority of the Saint-Laurent population tried to adapt to changing circumstances. Some, however, much to the irritation of the Oblates, seemed to be continuing their apparently nomadic lifestyle:

> La population de Saint-Laurent est composée presque exclusivement de Métis qui habitent les bords du lac. Ils se sont bâti des maisons aux environs de la mission et cultivent chacun un petit morceau de terre. Anciens chasseurs de la forêt, ils gardent encore leurs vieilles habitudes et passent plusieurs semaines a poursuivre le gibier. Il y en a un certain nombre qui ne s'éloignent jamais de la mission et qui vivent du produit de leur jardin et de la pêche, que le voisinage du lac leur permet toujours d'exercer... Encore que la langue française soit généralement comprise par la population du lac, cependant les Pères prêchent assez souvent en sauteux.[58]

*The Saint-Laurent population is composed nearly exclusively of Métis liv-
ing along the lakeshore. They have built houses near the mission and all
cultivate a small piece of land. Former hunters of the forests, they keep to
their old habits and spend several weeks each year hunting game. A certain
number of them never leave the vicinity of the mission and live from the produce of their gardens and from the fisheries that the vicinity of the lake
allows them always to practice… Even though the French language is generally understood, the Fathers often give their sermons in Saulteaux.*

After 1870 the Oblate missionaries displayed great energy attempting to
homogenise, sedentarise and agriculturise[59] the adult population[60] and transform
their children into good Catholic francophones.[61] The prognosis for both endeavours was not encouraging. Priests continually complained how the majority of Lake
Manitoba Métis lacked interest in farming[62] and were "fascinated" with fishing and
wintering in the north; both tended to conflict with agricultural pursuits.[63]

The missionaries' attempt to instill good "Catholic" behaviour in the local population was also not encountering much success. Basic religious practices, such as
baptizing dying infants,[64] were not actively observed even in reasonably well-to-do
families:

Quelque temps avant mon voyage à Saint-Boniface, à la Pointe des
Chênes, ils avaient laissé mourir un enfant sans baptême, l'enfant
de Baptiste Chartrand et de Marie Mezieprit [Messiapit].[65]

*Some time before my trip to Saint-Boniface, they had let a child die without
the benefit of the sacrament of baptism. This was the child of Baptiste
Chartrand and of Marie Mezieprit [Messiapit].*

Even the more educated families originating from the Red River Settlement,
such as the Delarondes, who had been held in high esteem by the clergy prior to
1870, began coming into conflict with the missionaries. The major point of con-
tention appears to have been marital arrangements:

Dans ma dernière lettre, je vous disais un mot de la pauvre Sophie
Morin, femme de William Linkster. D'après tout ce que j'ai pu voir
et juger par moi-même, voici l'histoire. William cède sa femme à
Paul Delaronde qui est parti avec elle dans la prairie ou pour
quelque endroit dans le Nord. William, dit-on, s'en va prendre
une autre à la Baie des Canards.[66]

*In my last letter, I wrote a word about poor Sophie Morin, wife to William
Linkster. From all that I have heard and can judge for myself, here is the
story. William gave his wife to Paul Delaronde, who has gone on the
prairies or somewhere north with her. William, they say, is going to Duck
Bay to get himself another one.*

The religious and secular education of children was also not progressing as the
missionaries had hoped. Saint-Laurent appears to have set up some sort of formal

school early in 1871, as opposed to the priest occasionally teaching a class. At some point in 1871, as many as 50 children were attending classes. The school commissioners were from the old trading element of the community—Louis Delaronde, Paul Chartrand and Joseph Lavallée. These traders appear to have sincerely wished to see their children educated. Despite the cooperative effort to mould the next generation, "problems" that had always plagued the missionaries persisted:

> La difficulté capitale contre laquelle viennent souvent se briser, ici comme dans quelques autres localités, tout zèle et bonne volonté des maîtres, consiste dans la langue. Le Cris et le Sauteux est parlé en famille, et l'enfant apprend a l'école une langue quasi nouvelle qu'il oublie presque une fois entré chez lui. La langue en effet entre pour beaucoup dans les habitudes et le genre d'idées d'un peuple. Or le Cris et le Sauteux est essentiellement la langue de la vie nomade du bois et de la prairie.[67]

> *The greatest difficulty, here and elsewhere, against which all efforts fail, whatever the good will and enthusiasm of the teacher, has to do with language. Cree and Saulteaux are spoken at home and the child goes to school to learn a language that is nearly foreign and which he tends to forget once home. Language has a great influence on the customs and mentality of a people. And Cree and Saulteaux are the languages of a nomadic existence in the woods or on the prairie.*

The Church in general had an ambivalent attitude towards most of the Lake Manitoba residents. Though the clergy obviously did not approve of many of these Métis' "nomadic" non-agrarian activities, they counted on them for a steady supply of fish to comply with the numerous meatless days found in the Catholic calendar. For example, in 1873, the Saint-Laurent fishermen supplied the convent and the archbishop's house with over 2,000 whitefish.[68]

The growing presence, increased activity and pervasive ideological bias of the Catholic clergy, along with the emergence of an increasingly market agrarian economy, would further divide and diversify the population of the Saint-Laurent area. In the crucial years between 1870 and 1881, some families once labelled Métis would begin the lengthy process of merging either into the "white" dominant society or into the northern "Indian" treaty population. Such divergent identities were partly the result of current political and economic constraints, but were also formed by past lifestyles and, perhaps, personal preferences. Chapter 3 will discuss the emergence of clear-cut class divisions that caused, or reinforced, changing ethnic identities.

CHAPTER 3

The Crucial First Decade, 1871–1881

AFTER 1870, DIVISIONS EXISTING WITHIN THE Lake Manitoba population continued to grow and new splits appeared. The different lifestyles of the residents were increasingly interpreted in a racist manner. The Oblates "whitened" those of their charges who were turning to more sedentary, approved, pursuits. A typical example is Abraham and Cécile (Larivière) McLeod. Although Abraham McLeod was a Métis born at Duck River and raised in the Saulteaux village, he and his Athabaskan Métis wife seem to have made a concerted effort to conform to the priests' wishes. The 1868 famine census reported that they possessed four horses, an ox, three cows and four calves. On this same census, the McLeods reported usually planting five bushels of potatoes, giving them an average annual harvest of 160 bushels. They were not considered indigent by the church authorities.

Abraham McLeod laid claim to a river lot in Oak Point and apparently lived there for the greater part of the year. The Oblates mention them several times in their correspondence in glowing terms for their "bonne conduite et bons offices."[1] At the death of Cécile, Brother Mulvihill gave her his highest accolade:

> It may be added that Mrs. McLeod had been both tall and strong
> and good looking and resembled a French Canadian rather than
> a half-breed. She spoke French, English, Cree and Sauteux.[2]

But were the Métis who continued in their seasonal migratory moves unwilling or unable to adapt themselves? The correspondence of Fathers Camper, Lestanc and McCarthy would seem to suggest a third alternative. Traders and their families were still going up to Duck Bay to winter, but more and more Métis not involved in dairy farming were heading *au large* to engage in large-scale commercial fishing activities. It was the emergence of new economic opportunities and not simply a reluctance to change that was anchoring many Métis in their peregrinations.[3] Fishing on whatever scale was an activity practised by all Lake Manitoba residents, whether traders, aspiring farmers or hunter-gatherers. In the 1870s several of the northern Métis residents, especially those with no claim to a river lot, seem to have been willing to go quite far afield in search of a catch on a network of lakes they were familiar with.

Based on comments made in the Oblate correspondence, there seems to have been a fairly set pattern to the post-1870 seasonal displacements made by the Saint-Laurent and Oak Point inhabitants. According to Father Camper, all able-bodied men left the settlement in August for Manitoba House (*Poste Manitoba*) on the northern part of the lake. It is unclear if they were fishing, trapping, or trading. They would return to spend the better part of September in Saint-Laurent and Oak Point. In October, many would depart again, some to winter in Duck Bay, others to engage in autumn fishing "un peu au-dela du poste Manitoba."[4] As the excerpt below indicates, the pre-1870 practice of the free traders leaving their Métis wives behind and wintering in the north with an "Indian" wife persisted. The fact that the people involved are from the extended French-speaking Delaronde family, highly regarded by the Oblates in the 1850s and 1860s, points to the usefulness of two wives for Métis involved in the Native trade:

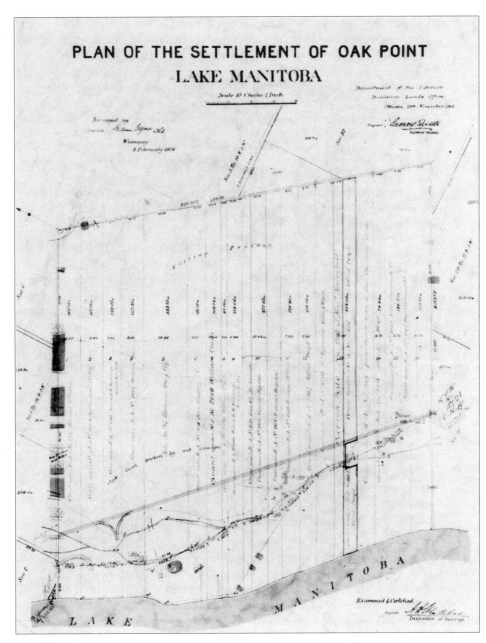

PAM N6451

Map made by William Wagner of his re-survey of Oak Point, Manitoba, in the early 1880s.

La mort de Julie Morin [Morelle] femme de Louison Delaronde. Elle laisse après elle bien de pauvres petits enfants, et entre autre deux petites besonnes qu'elle a nourrie pendant un an... Louison n'est pas encore revenu de son hivernement. Il ne connaît pas encore le coup terrible qui vient de le frapper. Pauvre Louison! Il a besoin que le bon Dieu lui fasse pitié à lui aussi. Puisse cette épreuve lui toucher le coeur et le ramener à son devoir.[5]

The death of Louison Delaronde's wife, Julie Morin [Morelle]. She leaves behind many poor young children including two little girl twins she nursed for a whole year... Louison has not yet returned from his winter camp so he does not yet know the terrible blow he has suffered. Poor Louison! He needs to have the good Lord take pity on him. May this hardship touch his heart and return him to his duty.

Fishermen spending several months in fishing camps on Lake Winnipegosis in the 1870s also took up this practice of dual marital arrangements.

The October leave-taking by the Lake Winnipegosis and Duck Bay *hivernants* seems to have been quite a tumultuous affair for Saint-Laurent and Oak Point. It was a time of weddings and rejoicing, much to the chagrin of the ecclesiastical authorities:

Hier, Isaie Pritchard, fils du défunt François Pritchard,* a pris pour espouse Julie Boucher fille du vieux Paul Boucher dit Lamalice.** A cette occasion et comme préparatif de départ pour l'hivernement, quelques'uns ont voulu faire des libations en l'honneur de Bacchus ... j'ai eu le triste avantage de voir de mes propres yeux non pas des sans-culottes, mais des sans-chemises.[6]

Yesterday, Isaie Pritchard, the son of the late François Pritchard, married old Paul Boucher dit Lamalice's daughter, Julie Boucher. For this occasion, along with the general preparation for the departure for the wintering areas, a few decided to offer libations in the honour of Bacchus ... I saw with my very eyes the sad spectacle not of "sans-culottes" but [of men] without shirts.

In November another Saint-Laurent and Oak Point contingent of Métis would leave once again to fish and trap in the Cygne River[7] and farther up the lake.[8] The autumn fishing catch could be quite substantial, since in November 1872 the Saint-Laurent fishermen were supplying the Archdiocese and convents with 2,000 white fish. The following November they supplied 1,800 fish to the religious authorities at the price of three (large) fish for one shilling.[9] Not all autumn and winter fishing

---

* Prichard also appears as "Ressard" and "Richard." François Richard was a French Canadian H.B.C. interpreter married to a Saulteaux women named Marguerite.

** He was the son of Paul and Françoise (St-Germain) Boucher *dit* Lamalice. He was married to Louise Marcellais.

---

would be so successful. If the fishermen were unable to catch enough to sell, they would have difficulty buying food (especially flour) for themselves and their families. Of course, the poor catch would most affect those who kept no animals and did no gardening. These Freemen Métis were subsistence fishermen.

As the following excerpts indicate, a majority of families on the south shores of Lake Manitoba in the 1870s still fell into the Freemen category. They did not engage in any form of gardening and husbandry. Métis who did garden and raise a few cattle were in a different position because, rather than buying all of their supplies from merchants, they could subsist at least partially on surpluses they produced. Also, they had an alternate source of income if fish yields or prices were poor. However, in the 1870s, farming was still an occupation that brought uncertain returns. Farmers periodically lost crops through frost, locusts or drought and would be forced, along with the full-time fishermen, to take up hunting and gathering:

> Je ne pense pas qu'aucun habitant du lac fasse aucune demande au Comité de Secours. C'est sans doute le meilleur parti. Ils peuvent facilement s'en passer. Habitué maintenant à la farine, ils trouvent dur de ne pas en avoir. Mais les petits brochets et les lièvres, sans donner grande force, laissent vivre et empêchent de mourir.[10]

> *I do not believe any of the lakeshore settlers will make any requests to the Emergency Aid Committee. It is probably the best course of action. They can easily do without. Now accustomed to flour, they find it hard not to have any. But, the small pikes and hares, without giving much strength, allow one to live and resist death.*

Over the winter several Saint-Laurent and Oak Point heads of families would be actively ice fishing, some going as far north as Dog River:

> Pierre Chartrand part demain pour aller faire la chasse du côté de la Rivière Poule d'Eau. Il y aurait dit-on bien du pelu dans les parages. Plus loin que la Pointe de Chênes à la Rivière du Cygne, les gens prennent bien du poisson blanc sous la glace. Quelques uns des habitants de Saint-Laurent ont pris cette direction. D'autres sont allés faire la pêche au Poste Manitoba. Aussi aujourd'hui il y avait peu d'hommes à la messe.[11]

> *Pierre Chartrand leaves tomorrow to hunt in the area of the Water Hen River. Apparently there are fur-bearing animals there. A bit beyond Oak Point, at the Swan River [creek], people are catching whitefish under the ice. Some of the Saint-Laurent settlers have headed in that direction. Others have gone to fish at Manitoba House. Therefore, today, there were few men in church.*

Spring would be a time for duck and muskrat hunting in the marshes that surrounded the mission. Again some would venture a bit further to Delta Marsh and Shoal Lake (*Lac Plat*).[12] The more settled families would plant small gardens and potato patches. Grasshoppers and frost were frequent calamities.[13] Several of the summer months were spent haying by the families who had livestock. As previously noted, Saint-Laurent was known for its natural hay lands.

These were the general economic activities in and around the shores of Lake Manitoba during the 1870s. But not all the Métis families were leading similar lifestyles. Four major groups were coalescing around social-economic distinctions first noted in the 1850s and 1860.[14] The first group, much approved by the clergy, was composed of Métis families who seemed determined to hang on to at least a portion of their land claims and to occupy their lots on a year-round basis.[15] The Chaboyers, the Ducharmes, the Boyers, some members of the Lavallée and Chartrand clans, and the McLeods of Oak Point, though continuing their trading and fishing activities around the lake, were spending more time in the Saint-Laurent and Oak Point area.

The second group was composed of the free traders. The Pangmans and Sayers no longer appear to have been involved in the Lake Manitoba trade network, or at least they were no longer based in the south end of the lake. But members of the Delarondes,[16] and some members of the Chartrand, Lavallée and perhaps the Monkman families, were and would continue trading in the 1880s. For example, in January 1885 William Chartrand, "merchant," accompanied by his wife Sophie Genaille, would serve as witness to a baptismal ceremony in Duck Bay.[17] His cousin, Michel Chartrand, was a clerk for the Hudson's Bay Company in the same area.[18] Another Michel Chartrand was trading in the Waterhen area for George Fisher.[19] These traders would continue their annual excursions north, sometimes taking with them their "Métis" families[20] or sometimes leaving them behind to rendezvous with their "Indian" families.

The priests' attitude was hardening towards this situation in the 1870s. From being "son autre femme" or "sa seconde femme," these northern women were now designated as "sa concubine" and when offspring were baptised they were listed as illegitimate, given their mother's last name and, increasingly, the father's name was not even listed in the parish registry. The lists of witnesses and godparents can sometimes give a clue to whose family these children were related. But, the tracing of the northern families becomes difficult since the priests increasingly refer to second wives as "those" women, rarely mentioning a first name and practically never a surname.

The third group were the hunting and gathering nomadic Métis, many of whom (whole families) went up in the traders' barges every autumn to winter on Lake Winnipegosis. They were Métis who pursued what could be called a more "traditional" or "Indian" lifestyle. But even these Freemen were fragmented into different groups. In the 1870s several families were choosing not to winter on the lakeshore but rather in the Riding Mountain area on the banks of the White Mud River, just as they had occasionally done in the past before the difficult 1860s. Bison and other large animals would be in plentiful supply until about 1874 when, according to Father Lestanc, OMI, after two years of frenetic killing and "gaspillage insensé d'animaux et de viande," hunger struck.[21] The Métis were no longer killing solely for meat and marrow; a lucrative market for bison robes was developing. The thick leather was used to make straps for industrial machinery. In their own ways, both the Métis and the bison contributed to the industrial revolution in North America.

It is clear some of these Riding Mountain *hivernant* families were from the Lake Manitoba-Winnipegosis area,[22] but others were Freemen from the Dakotas and farther west, such as the families of Antoine Gladu, James Whiteford, André Salomon, and Gabriel Azur.[23] In the mid-1870s some would come to settle "permanently" in the Saint-Laurent area at the invitation of Father Camper.[24] One such extended family was the Desjarlais. They had, for several years, made occasional visits to the mission area but their focus of activity had very much been the prairies (trading and bison hunting) prior to 1870.[25] Only one Desjarlais, Stanislav, would make a claim to an Oak Point river lot in 1872. Though several Desjarlais would eventually settle permanently in the Lake Winnipegosis area, a branch would move to Saint-Laurent and pursue a hunting-and-gathering life. Antoine Desjarlais[26] arrived in *La Mission* sometime in the 1870s and married Marie, the daughter of Joseph and Josèphte (Cadotte) Chartrand. He and his son, Joseph, lived out their lives as hunters and guides well into the 20th century.[27]

A fourth group that emerged after 1870 was composed of Métis families choosing to reside permanently in Duck Bay and the adjacent Indian reserve. They identified more and more with the surrounding Saulteaux population. There are tenuous indications that some of these families had initially resided on Lake Winnipegosis before coming to Saint-Laurent,[28] but for the majority of the hunting and trading families the Duck Bay area was "home" only for the winter. After 1870, missionary correspondence mentions Métis families who spent all their time in the north.[29] In the 1870s, Father Simonet was speaking with dismay of French Métis on the southern shores of Lakes Manitoba and Winnipegosis who were becoming "Indianised":

> La seule chose qui fait peine, c'est de constater que les petits enfants des vieux Canadiens dont les parents portent encore des noms français comme le chef Mousseau [Morrisseau] les conseillers Levasseurs et Antoine Beaulieu à Sandy Bay, les Genaille, Richard Ledoux de la Rivière aux Épinettes, ne parlent pas français. Et pourtant les parents ne parlent quère que le sauvage et ne comprennent que très peu d'anglais.[30]

> *The one thing that saddens me is to realise that the grandchildren of the old "Canadiens" whose parents still carry French surnames, such as chief Mousseau [Morrisseau], the council members Levasseurs and Antoine Beaulieu in Sandy Bay, the Genailles and Richard Ledoux of Pine River, speak no French. Yet the parents speak mostly Indian and understand little English.*

While the local population was being sorted out, the religious authority structure in the area was organising and affirming itself. In 1873 a full-sized church replaced the small chapel built in 1857. At least four Oblate fathers and brothers were residing in the monastery parsonage, looking after the "welfare" of the Lake

A photograph of the Saint-Laurent religious complex, taken in the early 20th century.

Manitoba residents. In 1875 a sturdier school building was erected near the church and the priests began a long-term campaign aimed at convincing parents to send their children to school—a school directly controlled by church authorities. By 1881 these same authorities were firmly in control of both the spiritual and the temporal matters of the area as one of their own, Brother Mulvihill, was appointed as the first administrator of the newly created municipality of Saint-Laurent.[31] The visibility and power of the Oblates in the area is truly startling to 21st-century researchers. In 1887 Mgr. Taché would proudly describe the temporal aspects of the mission of Saint-Laurent as follows:

> Ils [Oblates] possèdent 3,500 acres (ou 1,400 arpents) de terres estimés modestement par eux à 22,000 francs. Les constructions diverses ont au moins la valeur qu'ils leur attribuent, c'est à dire 34,000 francs, et leur magnifique troupeau de bétail de choix ferait honneur aux écuries d'un prince, quoi qu'il ne soit évalué par les propriétaires que de 6,000 a 7,000 francs.[32]

> *The Oblates own 3,500 acres of land modestly estimated by them as worth 22,000 francs. They value their buildings at 34,000 francs, which must be their minimum worth. Their magnificent herd of cattle would do honour to a prince's barn even though they assign to it only a value of 6,000 to 7,000 francs.*

1881 Manitoba Census					
Woodlands					
Heads of Household	Age	Occupation	People in household	School Age Children	Attending School
CHARTRAND					
Paul (I)	80	?	2	0	0
Paul (II)	42	hunter	9	4	0
Louis (II)	40	hunter	10	6	5
Norbert (II)	24	hunter	4	0	0
Antoine (II)	49	2 hunters	9	4	2
Baptiste (II)	35	hunter	4	2	0
PIERRE (I)	65	**hunter**	5	2	0
Napoléon (II)	25	hunter	2	0	0
Michel (II)	29	trader	6	2	0
Pierre (II)	30	farmer	5	2	0
Totals			56	22	7
LAVALLÉE					
BAPTISTE	80	N/A	4	0	1
Baptiste (I)	40	hunter	9	6	0
Joseph (I)	45	hunter	12	5	3
Michel (I)	32	hunter	6	2	0
André (I)	35	hunter	9	4	4
Totals			40	17	8
PANGMAN					
PIERRE	58	**hunter**	4	1	0
Michel (I)	28	**laborer**	4	0	0
Totals			8	1	0
Winnipegosis					
CHARTRAND					
BAPTISTE (I)	66	**farmer**	8	6	0
William (II)	30	hunter	6	2	0
Pierre (II)	24	2 hunters	4	0	0
MICHEL (I)	56	**farmer**	10	6	0
Pierre ?	40	**farmer**	7	3	0
Totals			35	17	0

By 1881, the year of the second federal census, the inhabitants of the southern shores of Lake Manitoba were integrating further into the provincial, national and international economies. Outside observers to the area in the 1880s stated that the residents of Oak Point and Saint-Laurent still lived mostly by fishing and hunting.[33] In a sense this is true. The northern salt works had closed and the fur trade was declining in importance, thus limiting the opportunities and options open to the trading element. However, data collected by the Department of Agriculture indicates that, despite what outsiders thought, the inhabitants of Saint-Laurent and Oak Point were embarking on a slow transition to cattle raising and mixed farming. In 1881 there were still only 34 acres under cultivation in the entire municipality, but enumerators counted 146 cattle (including oxen), 30 pigs, 49 horses and one sheep.[34] In the next two years the numbers would grow to 50 acres cultivated, 150 cattle, 22 pigs, 63 horses, but no sheep.[35]

The author hoped that the 1881 census would indicate in what *major* endeavour each family occupied itself in the early 1880s. However, the vast majority of heads of families listed for Saint-Laurent were simply labelled "hunters"; few traders and farmers were enumerated. Equally startling, a majority of the Métis listed as living in the Lake Winnipegosis-Duck Bay area declared themselves to be farmers. Fishing is simply not mentioned. An excellent example of these tendencies is the Chartrand family (see 1881 Manitoba Census Chart, next page). This apparently contradictory evidence does not necessarily refute claims of growing economic diversification within the Saint-Laurent-Oak Point population. The key variable was the season in which the censuses were taken in Saint-Laurent and on Lake Winnipegosis. The Saint-Laurent census was taken in May and June 1881, a time of year when several heads of household would engage in duck hunting in nearby marshes, independent of their other activities. The southern half of Lake Winnipegosis was canvassed between July and October 1881, when many of the year-round residents would be engaged in haying for the livestock (mostly horses). It would seem that most respondents simply listed as occupation the current activity that they were actively engaged in at the time of the census. For example, Joseph Chaboyer and his wife, Nancy Bonneau, were registered twice—once in Saint-Laurent, where he is listed as being a hunter, and again, later, in the Duck Bay area where he is designated as a farmer.

The people who spent significant time on the shores of Lake Winnipegosis would be, as noted above, busy in late summer cutting wild hay for their animals, and perhaps tending small gardens and potato patches. Such activities may have sufficed for the census taker to list them as "farmers." Being so far from any substantial markets, it is unlikely any of these people would be involved in commercial agriculture. Farming was already a difficult endeavour for people located in Saint-Laurent, 150 km to the south.

It should be noted that the census takers probably missed several Saint-Laurent families who were still in their winter quarters on Lake Winnipegosis in May and June of 1881.[36] Travelling was extremely difficult and dangerous in the spring because of ice break-up on the lakes. The census takers arriving in Duck Bay in July would again miss these hivernants because, by that time, the *hivernant* Métis had travelled by barge to their summer headquarters in Saint-Laurent.[37]

Still, not quite all the Saint-Laurent residents listed in the census declared themselves to be "hunters" in the spring of 1881, and the exceptions are interesting. From the Chartrand clan one member declared himself a farmer: Pierre Chartrand, age 30, son of Pierre Sr. and Marie Pangman. He was married to Elise Delaronde, daughter of Louis Delaronde and Judith Morin. His brother, Michel Chartrand Jr., married to Isabelle Ledoux,[38] listed trading as his occupation. In the late 1870s he had been managing a Hudson's Bay Company store in the parish of Saint-Laurent.[39] All the other Chartrand men (eight in total) declared hunting to be their occupation. Even important men such as the freighter-trader Baptiste Chartrand, husband of the "Indian" Mary Messiapit, stated his occupation as hunting.[40]

The five Lavallée men interviewed by the census takers all declared themselves to be hunters. The emphasis on hunting is quite startling since the Lavallées were one of the Lake Manitoba trading families that took an early interest in farming. In normal times, they collectively planted 12 bushels of potatoes,[41] which would have given an average yearly crop of 384 bushels. Even Baptiste Lavallée Jr., who harvested 21 bushels of potatoes in 1868, was listed as a hunter in the census of 1881.

Pierre Pangman, the grandson of a prominent NWC bourgeois, and son of a notable Métis Freeman-trader, was simply listed as a "hunter" in the census of 1881. Yet he was one of the earliest inhabitants in the area and, in the 1850s, the Pangmans and the Sayers were the only two families who had built wood houses in the area. Pierre Pangman's son Michel was listed as a labourer.

The Ducharmes, former residents of the Saulteaux village, had initially made two land claims in 1872. By 1881, there were five Ducharme households, comprised of seven adult men declaring a trade, living in the Saint-Laurent-Oak Point area. Moise Ducharme, who in 1872 was co-listed as an occupant (Lot 5) by surveyor William Wagner, was described as a hunter-carpenter. Baptiste Ducharme (age 66) who, according to the HBC register, lived on Lot 9, was described as a farmer. His married, live-in son, Corbert, declared himself to be a hunter. Louis Ducharme (age 64), claimant to Lot 7 (which eventually was sold to the Oblate Fathers), was described as a cartmaker and his live-in 23-year-old son, Pierre, was a hunter. Both Baptiste and Louis were listed as "indigents" in 1868 and as not usually putting in a crop. The last two Ducharmes, Jacques and Jean, are listed as hunters. It is interesting, for the Ducharme family at least, that adult men listed as "hunters" tended to be relatively young.[42]

The Richard family, of Freemen origin, also had five heads of households residing in Saint-Laurent in 1881. Pierre Richard (age 65) was listed as a carpenter along with three others of his relatives—François (age 45), St-Pierre (age 33), and Isaie (age 30).[43] Perhaps they had been involved in a building project at the time of the census. The fifth, listed as a hunter, was Pierre Richard, the son of widow Marguerite (François) Richard. His parents were the original claimants to lot 19 of Saint-Laurent. Interestingly, all seven Desjarlais male heads of family listed in the 1881 census were described as hunters.

The work description of the families having come up from the southern Métis parishes emphasised hunting to a lesser degree. Of the five Chaboyer heads of family listed in 1881, two claimed to be farmers.[44] A third, Pierre Chaboyer, declared himself to be a trader. The last two, Norbert and Joseph, claimants to Lots 12 and 15 (Saint-Laurent) were listed as hunters. The Chaboyers were a well-to-do Saulteaux village family. The patriarch was Louis Chaboyer, married to Louise Chartrand, and in 1843 he possessed three mares, a bull, two cows and two calves. The family made periodic trading trips to the shores of Lake Manitoba in the early 1860s prior to the definitive move by several of its members in 1867–68. The trader, Pierre Chaboyer, and his wife Philomène de Montigny, had a child baptized in Saint-Laurent in the spring of 1864, a time of the year when the hunting and gathering elements would have been camping at the mission. The same year, Joseph Chaboyer and Nancy Bonneau also had their child baptized at the Saint-Laurent mission (time of year uncertain). According to an affidavit in the Saint-Laurent river lot files, though living most of the year in Saint-François-Xavier, Joseph and Nancy Chaboyer had been coming seasonally to a specific location (Lot 15) in the Saint-Laurent mission.[45] This was a man listed as non-indigent in 1868. He had a house, a barn and at least one-third of an acre in crop in 1870. His lot was patented in his name in 1876. For such a Métis to be listed as a hunter in 1881 gives weight to the argument that many lakeshore residents stated their occupation as the activity in which they were engaged on the day the census was taken.

Blacksmith Pierre Boyer, with his wife Genevieve Martin, successfully claimed Lot 24 in Saint-Laurent in the 1870s. Yet, during 1868 they were listed as being indigent residents of Saint-Laurent, even though they normally planted 10 bushels of potatoes yearly.[46] Though absent from the 1870 census, they reappear in 1881 when Pierre Boyer's 20-year-old son, Louis, is listed as a hunter.[47]

In 1881 there were only two representatives of the Delaronde trading family left in Saint-Laurent. The first Delaronde head of family is described as a farmer, and the other as a livestock raiser. The Goulet family had two representatives at the mission, one who declared himself to be a farmer and one a hunter. The Nabase (dit Lecris) family, originally from Red River, had only one representative in Saint-Laurent and Oak Point in 1881—James, described as a hunter. Finally, the ageing Louis Carrière, husband of Julie Marchand and the successful claimant of Lot 17 in Saint-Laurent, also was listed as a blacksmith in 1881.

A "new" family of uncertain origin, the Guiboches, appears on the 1881 census. They eventually became quite numerous in the Saint-Laurent-Oak Point area. In 1881 Edouard Guiboche, husband of a woman named Larose (Rosella dit Larose), is listed as a hunter. Edouard Guiboche may have been the son or grandson of Louis Guiboche, a Métis trader and freighter mentioned by Marcel Giraud.[48] A respondent born in 1909 noted that she remembered the "old" Guiboche family members as Saulteaux-speakers, and that someone had told her that the Guiboche family originally had come down from the north.[49] Other families listed in the 1870 census appear not to have been present in the spring of 1881.

Given the apparent problem with how the respondents *perceived* the occupation question, not much irrefutable information on the changing and diverging economic pursuits within the Métis population can be extracted from the 1881 census. There does seem to be a slightly greater tendency for the heads of family originating from the southern parishes to declare themselves farmers but, because so many families are missing from the census, this cannot be stated with certainty. There also seems to be a slight tendency for younger heads of family to have declared themselves to be hunters.

Not surprisingly, five Chartrand men and their families are listed as residing on the shores of Lake Winnipegosis in 1881. This important trading family always had close business and family ties with the Duck Bay area. Some of its members had opted, prior to 1870, to reside there more or less permanently. For example, though listed in the 1870 census as residents of Saint-Laurent, and making a claim on Lot 1 in 1872, Michel (age 56) and Marguerite (Pangman) Chartrand had built a house in Duck Bay in 1858.[50] In the summer of 1881 they were residing in Duck Bay and Michel Chartrand declared himself to be a farmer. Two other Chartrands, polled in Duck Bay in the summer of 1881—Baptiste (age 66) and Pierre Sr. (age 40)—also stated their occupation as farming. Only the youngest Chartrand heads of family, residing in Duck Bay—Pierre (age 24)[51] and William (age 30)—were hunters.

Of the families originating from Red River that were listed by the census taker as residing in Duck Bay, the most prominent were the Delarondes. Given their extensive contacts with the area through trading activities over the previous three decades, one would expect that some of their members would be spending the summer on Lake Winnipegosis. One Delaronde head of family is listed as a farmer, the second as a freighter, and the third as a labourer. The fourth Delaronde listed in the 1881 Lake Winnipegosis census is listed as "Indian" hunter (as opposed to "French" hunter). It is impossible to know if being "Indian" or "French" was a self-perception on the part of the respondent or the opinion of the census taker. Since the 1881 census does not give the names of the fathers of the heads of family, it is impossible to know how closely related the "Indian" hunter Pierre Delaronde was to the Red River Delarondes.

Two Duck Bay Chaboyer heads of family, Antoine (age 35) and Joseph (age 36), gave farming as their occupation. One Joseph Desjarlais head of family was residing in Duck Bay in 1881. He is described as married to a "Sioux" woman and being, interestingly enough, a hunter-farmer. The Richard and Sayer families each have one farming head of family dwelling on the shores of Lake Winnipegosis. The three Monkman (old salt-making family) adult men listed at Duck Bay in 1881 are described as hunter-farmers. Two Ducharmes are also listed as hunter-farmers. Interestingly, no Pangman head of family is listed for the Duck Bay area even though we know from other sources that some of their members had been residing there since the late 1850s.[52]

As previously suggested, the 1881 census is problematic. The census takers missed many families that we know from sources such as the ecclesiastical correspondence and the parish and missions register to be residing in either Duck Bay or the Saint-Laurent-Oak Point area in 1881. Also, the work description of the people polled makes little sense. Why would so many adult men be listed as farmers in Duck Bay while the Saint-Laurent and Oak Point area bristled with hunters? As mentioned above, the time of the survey and how people perceived the questions are two possible explanations for the anomalies. One observation that can be drawn from the survey is that it was mostly the old Lake Manitoba and the trading-oriented Delaronde families that were spending that summer on Lake Winnipegosis. Except for some members of the Chaboyer family,[53] the post-1867–68 Red River and Saint-François Xavier contingent seem to have been settling down in Saint-Laurent, an indication of their greater interest in pursuing an agrarian lifestyle (despite their being labelled "hunters" by the census takers).

The period between the censuses of 1881 and of 1891 was a period of rapid social change and increasing economic and ideological pressures for the Métis of Saint-Laurent and Oak Point. Prior to 1881, all the families that had settled in the region, even if they differed in material wealth and occupational pursuits, considered themselves to be "Métis," however the term might be defined. After 1881, settlers with funds began arriving in Saint-Laurent and Oak Point. They did not perceive themselves as Métis, were unsympathetic to traditional hunting and gathering pursuits, and were imbued with the late 19th-century views on miscegenation.[54] In the consequential decade of 1881–91, a marginal and destitute subclass, labelled Métis whatever its historical origins, developed in the Saint-Laurent-Oak Point area.

CHAPTER 4

Des "Étranges"[1] arrivent, 1881–1891

BETWEEN 1881 AND 1891 THE MÉTIS OF Saint-Laurent and Oak Point faced further changes in their economy and society. The lakeshore residents continued to experience the economic changes heralded by the arrival of southern Métis families in the late 1860s. The southern Métis were interested in commercial fishing and dairy farming and continued, between 1881 and 1891, to secure their holdings and to expand their farming and fishing activities. But, starting in the 1881–91 decade, both groups of Métis, the more settled southerners and the old Lake Manitoba Freemen and trading families, were faced with the arrival of Catholic French-speaking farming families, bringing prejudices mirroring those of the Oblates.

The Métis population increased steadily in the Saint-Laurent-Oak Point area between 1881 and 1891. The 1881 census listed approximately 390 "French" men, women and children born in the North-West Territories or Manitoba as residing in the "Woodlands" electoral district; most, presumably, concentrated in the two settlements. The 1886 census shows 414 Métis (no Indians) living in Townships 16 and 17 west of Shoal Lake that include the Saint-Laurent and Oak Point area. Métis families were also starting to settle a bit further north in their old fishing and hunting grounds at Swan Creek (*Rivière du Cigne*). At the time of the 1886 census there were 130 settled at Swan Creek, making a combined total of 544 Métis inhabiting the southeast shores of Lake Manitoba.[2] To this resident population were added a few French Catholic families (totalling about 37 people)[3] recruited directly from Québec or from the French-Canadian migrant population who had left Québec to work in the Massachusetts textile mills earlier in the century. Surprisingly, between 1881 and 1891 several titled families from France, who sought to escape political upheaval and to seek lucrative investment opportunities, also came to the Saint-Laurent area.

The Duc de Blacas arrived in Saint-Laurent in the spring of 1882. According to the parish's *Codex Historicus*, de Blacas bought 1,000 acres between Saint-Laurent and Oak Point, "the greater part of which belonged to Halfbreed minor children who could not give a clear title for about a year, hence he got a big reduction in price."[4] After building a stone house of "manorial" appearance the duke hired a Québécois, Ovide Lacoursière, to manage his interests.[5] Lacoursière arrived at the farm with a herd of quality milk cows purchased in the east and all the equipment necessary to install a cheese-making factory. By 1891 the French duke had 180 animals on his land, which had increased to 2.5 sections.[6]

In autumn of 1882 a compatriot of the duke, the Comte De Simencourt,[7] purchased near the duke's property a large tract of land he called the "ranch de Lisbyville."[8] Some details on the commercial activities of this count are known. By 1885 he had assembled a herd of 130 cattle and was involved in the large-scale production of butter.[9] He also had 200 sheep "de bonne race." In the summer of 1885 De Simencourt would cut 5,000 tons of hay to feed his livestock over winter. He also rented a stall in the public market of Winnipeg and the quantity of meat that he sold there would cause a temporary slump in prices in the largest city on the prairies.[10] The count and his family would stay in the Saint-Laurent area running their meat and cheese operations until the mid-1890s.

Less is known about the Duke de Blacas's economic endeavours. However, by 1883 his *métayer* (manager) Lacoursière had successfully launched his cheese-making operation. It was the first such commercial enterprise in the area. In 1884 Lacoursière was announcing his willingness to buy up all the surplus milk and cream in Saint-Laurent.[11] The cheese factory was surely a boost for the local families interested in dairy farming. This factory was in operation until 1891, when the duke, having made a lucrative marriage, opted to return to France.

A third nobleman, the Comte de Leusse, also ran a cheese-making operation for a short time in the 1890s. His presence was beneficial even to the non-farming Métis:

> Monsieur le comte de Leusse fait une grande charité à tous nos enfants d'école. Il leur donne et leur donnera pendant tout l'hiver le repas du midi, une bonne soupe chaude, du biscuit, de la viande, des pommes de terre. C'est intéressant de voir tous ces marmots fricoter et se régaler comme jamais de leur vie. Le résultat désiré est obtenu. L'assistance est plus régulière.[12]

> *Monsieur the count of Leusse is being very charitable towards our school children. He gives them, and will give them all winter, the noon meal composed of hot soup, biscuit, meat and potatoes. It is fascinating to see those youngsters eat as they have never eaten in their lives. The desired end is obtained. School attendance has become more regular.*

De Leusse's operations would eventually be taken over by a Québécois, Edmond Trudel,[13] who continued the cheese and butter factory with milk supplied by neighbouring farmers.

Finally, a fourth untitled but moneyed French family, the Viels, settled permanently in Saint-Laurent in 1891. In the 1901 census Louis Viel, head of the household, declared his profession to be that of "notary." With him were two unmarried adult sons, Raymond and Leonce, who were listed as farmers. One unmarried daughter, Margaret (age 28), declared her occupation to be teaching. This family ran a large dairy farm and cheese factory. All these cheese- and butter-making operations provided outlets for the dairy-oriented Métis, who themselves did not have sufficient land or capital to mount similar operations.[14]

The 1880s were a decade when the Métis involved in dairying were further integrated into the provincial economy.[15] They were now assured a steady market for their milk and cream at the local cheese and butter factories:

> Monsieur Sigfroid Lachance doit ouvrir une fromagerie ce printemps; ce sera la seconde que nous ayons [à Saint-Laurent]. M. Lachance a quarante vaches à lait qui lui appartiennent, sans compter que plusieurs de ses voisins doivent envoyer le lait de leurs vaches à sa fromagerie.[16]

> *Mr. Sigfroid Lachance is to open a cheese factory this spring; it will be the second one we have. Mr. Lachance owns forty milk cows and several of his neighbours are supposed to send their milk to his cheese factory.*

Prior to the rise of the local cheese and butter factories, farmers had to make their own butter, cut it into pound prints,[17] sell all they could locally, and haul the rest to Winnipeg at their own expense. Before the completion of the new highway in 1881 this was a long and arduous journey along the old ox-cart fur-trade trail. The Métis dairy farming families were encouraged in their endeavours by church authorities, and by 1887 Father Camper noted in a letter to Mgr. Taché that the baptismal records should probably list children of some Métis families as "white."[18]

Between 1881 and 1891, many members of the Lake Manitoba population pursued a life of hunting, gathering and fishing to the great dismay of the Oblates. The number of hunting and gathering families struck the Comte Louis de Turenne, passing through the mission in 1881:

> La mission de Saint-Laurent n'a pas plus de 400 habitants tous métis français et saulteaux vivant du produit de leur chasse et leur pêche. Malgré leurs efforts, les missionnaires n'ont pu arriver à les décider a cultiver le sol pourtant très fertile… Généralement les métis sont doux et paisibles, facile à instruire. Les familles sont très nombreuses… Malheureusement, il est presque impossible d'empêcher qu'ils emploient entre eux autre chose que le saulteaux et ils arrivent rarement à parler facilement une autre langue.[19]

> *The mission of Saint-Laurent has no more than 400 inhabitants, all French and Saulteaux Métis living from their hunting and fishing. Despite all their efforts, the missionaries have been unable to convince them to cultivate the soil even though it is quite fertile… By and large the Métis are soft spoken and peaceable, easy to instruct. The families are very large… Unfortunately, it is nearly impossible to stop them from using amongst themselves the Saulteaux language and they rarely learn to speak another language well.*

Many reasons prompted Métis families to continue in what were perceived by outsiders as "traditional" pursuits. Saint-Laurent was the buying and shipping point for all fish caught in Lake Manitoba and Lake Winnipegosis because of its southerly location on the lake and its proximity to a good highway to Winnipeg.[20] Also, the Saint-Laurent area continued to be an important fishing centre in its own right:

> Il y a sur les bords du lac une centaine de pêcheurs qui sont à l'œuvre depuis l'automne dernier et qui obtiennent de bons gages pour leur travail. On paie d'un à deux sous la livre pour le brochet livré sur glace. Le poisson est ensuite transporté à Raeburn et expédié de là aux États-Unis où il est en grande demande.[21]

> *There are on the shores of the lake approximately one hundred fishermen who have been working since last autumn and are getting good wages for their labour. They are paying one or two cents a pound for pike delivered on ice. The fish is than sent to Raeburn and from there to the United States, where it is in great demand.*

From Saint-Laurent, fish was sent overland to Winnipeg where freight trains transported it to various markets[22]:

> Le commerce de poisson augmente continuellement ici, un de nos marchands vient de recevoir l'ordre d'en envoyer trois chars à Chicago le plus tôt possible. Depuis le commencement de l'hiver l'on en a déjà envoyé 15 chars de la partie sud du lac. La petite rivière [Swan Creek] nous fait l'effet d'un marché tant sont nombreux les camps de pêcheurs qui accourent de tous les côtés.[23]

> *The fish trade increases continually here. One of our merchants has received the order to send three train carloads to Chicago as soon as possible. Since the beginning of winter we have already sent fifteen train carloads from the southern part of the lake. The little river [Swan Creek] has become a market to us with all the fishing camps there filled with fishermen from all over.*

As stated in the previous chapter, most families living in Saint-Laurent were involved in fishing to some degree. The crucial point was the relation between fishing and other economic pursuits. Members of several families (Chaboyer, Carrière, Delaronde) combined fishing with animal husbandry while others, the majority, continued hunting and gathering. Many reasons can explain the persistence of pre-1870 economic pursuits: the most obvious reason was the lack of capital and land necessary for building a dairy herd. But not all the reasons were negative; trapping as well as hunting and gathering could still occasionally have been lucrative. In the spring of 1881 (at the time of the census), for example, the price for muskrat pelts was at an all-time high[24]:

> Plusieurs familles sont même parties armes et bagages, hommes, femmes, enfants.[25] C'est une véritable richesse, année d'abondance pour nos pauvres gens. Si du moins ils savaient en profiter, s'ils pensaient à l'avenir et s'achetaient des instruments aratoires etc. afin de devenir plus tard des Habitants.[26]

> *Several families have left, men, women and children with all the necessities. It is true richness, an abundant year for our poor people. If only they knew how to profit from it. If they thought of the future and bought some farm tools so as to become one day "habitants" [peasants].*

Father Camper's disapproval of the reluctance of the hunting-and-gathering Métis to buy agricultural implements is surprising since he had noted that most of the Métis had no title to the land that they lived on. Also, however lucrative trapping and fishing activities could be in some years, the returns were usually only enough to meet ordinary living expenses and avoid debt:

> Mort aux rats! Eh! Qu'il s'en tue de ces rats et cependant pas encore assez pour payer toutes les dettes! Règle générale tous les printemps un bon nombre sont en peine. On a beau les avertir de prendre garde...[27]

*Death to the rats! Hey! So many rats are killed but still it is not enough to
pay off all the debts! As a general rule, by springtime many face hardships.
And yet we always warn them...*

Also, the hunting activities of the Freemen Métis continued to interfere with
attempts at gardening and crop growing. In the autumn of 1882, Father Camper,
in one of his frequent letters to Mgr. Taché, noted that while the missionaries and
some "worthy" families were busy harvesting potatoes and working their fields,
"others" were engaged in a "war to death" against ducks. Hundreds, apparently,
were shot daily.[28] Moose hunting also seemed to be an important autumnal activity
in the region until the 1890s.[29]

Some new activities were opening up for the non-farming Métis. In the summer
of 1881 Camper noted that some of the "restless" Métis were working for wages
constructing the railway in the Poplar Point area.[30] In addition, missionary letters
became increasingly filled with concerns about these Métis losing their souls while
working for Protestant farmers:

> [Religious] indifference due to contact of men and boys amongst
> a protestant population during the 3 months of the year when
> they go off to work the harvest at *least* to Portage la Prairie,
> Stonewall and elsewhere. Even whole families at times go and
> camp in the vicinity of these little towns where women and chil-
> dren remain while the men are far away at work in the fields or
> elsewhere. At times women and children hire to work or such in
> the towns.[31]

The missionaries' disapproval of non-farming families translated into active
efforts to recruit "white" French Catholic settlers and to relocate the hunting and
gathering element to the north (away from Protestant influence). Upon the arrival
of the Duc de Blacas, Father Camper would comment that he had been praying not
for nobility but for good examples of Catholic *habitants*[32] for the local population.[33]

Clearly the missionaries did not think that all the Saint-Laurent and Oak Point
residents would benefit from contact with the incoming farming settlers. The missionaries were frankly hostile and held little hope of turning the Freemen and
other hunting and gathering Métis into *habitants*. As early as the spring of 1880,
Father Camper was asking Mgr. Taché if he could permanently relocate himself to
the Indian settlement of Pine Creek on the shores of Lake Winnipegosis and not
the old Métis settlement of Duck Bay: "Je ne parle pas des vieux habitants de Saint-
Laurent, on sait depuis longtemps ce qu'ils valent."[34] All the disturbances occurring
in the parish[35] or the mission areas were blamed on these "fringe" Métis. The tone
of the written condemnations could be quite virulent:

> Les pauvres métis de la Baie des Canards se montrent et se mon-
> treront toujours ce qu'ils sont. Je les ai [?] fortement pour leur
> négligence et leur paresse. Quelles tristes gens! Les quelques
> sauvages qui demeurent encore au milieu d'eux souffrent de leur
> position et soupirent après le jour où ils pourront s'éloigner.[36]

> *The poor Métis of Duck Bay show themselves as they are and will always*
> *be. I have [?] strongly for the negligence and their indolence. What poor*
> *people! The few Indians who live amongst them suffer from their situation*
> *and hope for the day they can move away.*

Or again:

> Aux quatre coins de la paroisse il y a des personnes scandaleuses,
> femmes et filles perdues, qui font l'œuvre du démon et perdent
> les âmes. Elles sont vendues presque toutes d'ailleurs... Et toute
> cette mauvaise graine est du métis et du sauvage.[37]

> *At the four corners of the parish live scandalous people. Lost women and*
> *girls who do the work of the devil and lose souls. They are sold nearly all*
> *of them... And all this bad seed is Métis or Indian.*

It was the old Freemen families of Saint-Laurent and Oak Point that Father
Camper wished to see relocated in the north. In 1883, in a letter addressed to E.
McColl, the inspector of Indian Agencies, Camper urged the government to estab-
lish a reserve at Pine Creek (Lake Winnipegosis), arguing that many Saint-Laurent
families would then be inclined to relocate in that area.[38] He elaborated his propos-
al in a letter to Mgr. Taché in which he extolled the benefits of a reserve at Pine
Creek, because both the Indian population of Lake Winnipegosis and the "free"[39]
Métis population coming up from Lake Manitoba could organise and settle there.[40]
His plans appear to have been successful since, by 1901, Métis families having relocated near the Pine Creek reserve were petitioning the government to allow them
to "enter into treaty." According to Camper they were willing to abandon their
Métis scrip in exchange for treaty rights.[41]

Between 1881 and 1891, the old Lake Manitoba trading families were also facing changes and constraints. Those individuals who had opted to continue in commerce were dealing with increased competition in Saint-Laurent from itinerant
merchants.[42] Even the northern trade was not secure; by the end of the 1880s
steamboats had made their appearance on Lake Manitoba[43] and were taking over
some of the freighting business. Rival Winnipeg-based companies could now move
large amounts of trade goods north, faster and cheaper than their lakeshore com-
petitors. In the coming years some of these Métis traders would opt for a life based
on farming and fishing, others would relocate north,[44] and a third group would
continue to buy and sell either as independent traders or in the employ of
Winnipeg merchants.

The 1891 census indicates how the Saint-Laurent population was restructuring
near the turn of the century. However, it should be noted that all the caveats and
cautions applicable to the interpretation of the 1881 census apply to that of 1891.
It is still unclear how respondents perceived the questions put to them, especially
the crucial matter of "occupation." Also, the census takers went through the parish
of Saint-Laurent during a time when some *hivernants* had not yet returned,
between April 6 and May 30, 1891; others may have been absent due to egg gathering[45] or muskrat hunting.[46] A final problem with both the 1881 and 1891 federal

censuses is the quality of the microfilms. These manuscript sources were micro-filmed and then destroyed. The quality of the negatives is poor and several names on the list are simply illegible.

In 1891, in the expanded municipality of Saint-Laurent, there were approxi-mately 600 "Métis" and "French Canadians." Most still lived in log houses on the crowded lake lot settlements of Saint-Laurent and Oak Point. These two linear set-tlements were the most densely populated settlements in the whole Interlake.[47] By 1885 the missionary correspondence was noting the arrival of Québécois, Irish and Métis migrants to the Saint-Laurent area. The Métis migrants appear for the most part to have come from the more southerly parishes. Many relatively well-to-do Métis families were leaving the parishes of Saint-Boniface, Saint-Norbert,[48] Saint-François Xavier and Sainte-Agathe[49] in despair of ever getting their letters patent to the land they occupied. A few other families from the Lake Winnipegosis area were also relocating to Saint-Laurent.

Of the old Saint-Laurent trading families, the Pangmans and the Sayers on the south shores of Lake Manitoba were faring the least well in 1891. Only one Pangman was residing in the Saint-Laurent area in 1891. This was Catherine Pangman, a 65-year-old illiterate widow. The 1881 census had listed two Pangman heads of family, a hunter and a labourer. It is possible both were still simply hunt-ing and fishing in their winter quarters in 1891; or, they had permanently relocat-ed to the north. The importance of the Pangman family in the parish had been declining since the late 1860s and early 1870s. The focus of their social and eco-nomic activities had increasingly been the Duck Bay area.[50] The Sayers do not appear at all in the 1891 census. The Sayer family name is not mentioned anywhere in the archival record after the early 1880s.[51]

The third earliest family to be found in Saint-Laurent had been the Chartrand clan. Of the 10 adult heads of family (all males) listed in 1881, six plus one widow head of family were present in the 1891 parish of Saint-Laurent census. Four sons of deceased Paul and Josèphte (Cadotte) Chartrand were still residing in the parish: Paul, Norbert and Antoine were hunters and/or fishermen, with only Baptiste claiming to be a farmer. Two sons of Pierre and Marie (Pangman) Chartrand, Michel and Napoleon Chartrand, were also present. Michel, who in 1881 had declared his occupation to be trading, was now listed as a farmer. Surprisingly, Napoleon, first listed in 1881 as a 25-year-old hunter, was now listed as a 32-year-old teacher.[52] Pierre Chartrand, a farmer and storekeeper highly regard-ed by the Oblates, had died by 1891[53] but his wife, Elise, headed a household in 1891 composed of herself, three children, and two (Delaronde) boarders.[54]

Five new Chartrand households are listed in 1891. Three more children of Paul and Josèphte are listed residing in the parish. Pierre and Xavier are hunter-fishermen and Hermas is listed as being an armer (?) and general servant. Two sons of Pierre and Marie are settled in the vicinity of their parents' house. Baptiste is a farm labourer and Magloire is a hunter-fisherman. An indication of the unre-liability of the census taken in early spring is the absence of Pierre and Marie (Pangman) Chartrand who were listed in the 1870 and 1881 census and who had been in the area since the late 1850s. They were still residents of Saint-Laurent because, in October 1896, Father Camper mentioned them in a letter to Mgr. Langevin describing the preparation surrounding their golden wedding anniversary.[55] Though Camper describes Pierre and Marie Chartrand as Saint-Laurent's most venerable couple, he nevertheless goes on to comment, with some degree of satisfaction, that the Chartrand "clan" seemed to be dissolving in Saint-Laurent. This would be consistent with the somewhat slow increase (much below natural growth rates) of Chartrand heads of family in Saint-Laurent between 1881 and 1891, and the declining importance of independent fur traders on the south shores of Lake Manitoba.[56]

In sharp contrast to the Chartrands, all the Lavallées listed in 1881 were present in the 1891 census. In 1881, all five heads of household had declared themselves to be hunters. In 1891, André Lavallée (whose Lot 10 had been patented to the Oblates), husband to Elise Chaboyer, declared himself to be a farm labourer. Their adult unmarried sons declared themselves to be a farm labourer (Henry) and a hunter (Baptiste). Antoine, husband of Isabelle Chaboyer, continued to list hunting as his occupation. Old Baptiste Lavallée, husband to Louise Ducharme, was also a hunter, as was Joseph, husband of Angélique Campbell and partial owner of Lot 6. Michel and Elise Lavallée were now a hunting and fishing family. Their 13-year-old son, John, was described as an illiterate, salaried stable boy. A sixth Lavallée household, Baptiste Jr. and his wife Suzanne, who were mentioned in the relief lists (non-indigent) and in 1870 but not in 1881, resurfaced in 1891. Baptiste Jr. declared himself to be an illiterate hunter. Their daughter, Louise (age 21), was listed as a salaried cook and their son, Michel, was a hunter. Four new Lavallée heads of household also stated their occupation as hunting—Antoine (age 22), married to Henriette Nabes, Pierre (age 31), married to "Mary," John (age 28), married to Virginie Leclerc (age 24), and Joseph (age 27), married to Eloize Loyer (age 23), who combined hunting and fishing.

The four original families of Fond du Lac were not faring well in 1891. The Lavallées and the Chartrands continued to have several representatives in Saint-Laurent. Only two, Michel Chartrand married to Isabelle Ledoux and Napoleon Chartrand, listed in the 1891 census as married to "Angelique" (age 22),[57] appear to have integrated into "non-traditional" occupations. The first was a farmer and the other a teacher. Again, however, a note of caution must be voiced as to how the respondents perceived the "occupation" question.[58] This is also true for the other "early" families of Lake Manitoba.

Of the other known "early" families of Lake Manitoba, the Ducharmes in 1891 had seven heads of family listed. Three had appeared in the 1881 census; the most prominent, Jean-Baptiste Ducharme, the patentee for Lots 3 and 9, was once again listed as a "farmer." Jean and Jacques Ducharme were listed again as hunters but, in 1891, they also declared themselves to be fishermen. The four other Ducharme heads of family, whose ages vary from 25 to 50 years old, all declared themselves to be hunters and fishermen except for Maurice Ducharme, who was an unemployed carpenter. None of the Ducharmes listed in the Duck Bay area for 1881 are found in Saint-Laurent in the spring of 1891.

All five of the Richard heads of family listed in 1881 were also found in the 1891 census. Four declared themselves to be carpenters in 1881 and two, François and Pierre, declared the same occupation in 1891. The third, Isaie (age 41), married to Julie Boucher, claimed in 1891 to be a hunter. The fourth Richard family, Pierre and Isabelle (Chartrand) Richard, patentees of Lot 18, were not listed as a hunting and fishing family. By 1891 Pierre Richard was 74 years old and probably unable to do strenuous carpentry work. The widow, Marguerite (née Saulteaux) Richard, was listed as still residing in her Saint-Laurent home in 1891, but her son Pierre, the hunter, was not in Saint-Laurent that spring. Five other Richard heads of family, between 28 and 42 years of age, were listed in 1891. Three were noted as illiterate farm labourers and the other two as hunter-fishermen. There was one Richard family listed for Duck Bay in 1881, but the lack of a legible first name makes correlation impossible.

Only four Desjarlais heads of family, out of the seven listed in 1881, were found in the 1891 census. All four had been listed as hunters in 1881. In 1891, Stanislav Desjarlais, original claimant of Lot 10 in Oak Point, was listed as a farmer living in the *La Mission* area. Louis Desjarlais was dead by 1891 and his wife, Julia Chartrand was listed as head of family but no occupation was given. Antoine and Marie (Chartrand) Desjarlais formed a farm labouring family. Louis Desjarlais was a hunter-fisherman. No new Desjarlais family head was listed. The Desjarlais family pursued a life of hunting and gathering, coupled with occasional guiding work, right up to World War II. It is quite likely that, in the spring of 1891, most of the able-bodied Desjarlais men and their families were away hunting.

If the families who settled in Saint-Laurent from 1867 on are examined, it is the extended Chaboyer family which made the most land claims. Four of the five Chaboyers listed in 1881 were also present in 1891. Pierre Chaboyer, husband of Philomène de Montigny and successful claimant to Lot 16 (Saint-Laurent), had been listed as a trader in 1881. Ten years later he was a farmer. This was one of the families highly regarded by the clergy, and upon Pierre's death in May 1891 Father Camper would remark to Mgr. Taché that,

> Il y a une quinzaine de jours mourait à Saint-Laurent un de nos anciens et bons paroissiens Pierre Chaboyer, époux de Philomène de Montigny.[59]

> *Two weeks ago Pierre Chaboyer died in Saint-Laurent. Husband to Philomène de Montigny, he was one of our old and good parishioners.*

Ambroise Chaboyer, patentee to Lot 14, a farmer in 1881, was in 1891 described as a fisherman-hunter. Norbert Chaboyer, proprietor of Lot 12, was described as a hunter in 1881 and as a hunter-fisherman in 1891. Baptiste Chaboyer, a farmer in 1881, had sold his claim to Father Camper in the 1880s[60] and was not listed in the 1891 census. Joseph Chaboyer and his wife, Nancy Bonneau, listed in 1870 in Saint-Laurent and in 1881 in Duck Bay, were a hunting and fishing family residing once again in the parish of Saint-Laurent in 1891. The appearance and disappearance from the various censuses of the names of heads of families is not a surprising pattern. Some of the Chaboyer households, such as Antoine and Marie Chaboyer, not listed in 1870 or 1881 but found in the 1868 and 1891 lists, frequently wintered away from the parish in the northern fishing camps—*despite* their obvious concern for ownership of land. On May 1, 1882, Camper remarked in his letter to the Bishop:

> Rien de nouveau sinon la mort de la femme d'Antoine Chaboyer. Ella a eu les sacrements... La Bonne Providence arrange toujours toutes les choses pour le mieux. Les années précédentes cette famille se trouvait au loin.[61]

> *Nothing new here except the death of Antoine Chaboyer's wife. She received the last sacraments... The Good Lord arranges things for the best. In prior years this family was always away [wintering].*

Two other Chaboyer households were listed in the 1891 census, the first headed by a hunter-fisherman and the second by a farm labourer.

The old Saint-Boniface trading family, the Delarondes, still had only two heads of family listed in the 1891 census for Saint-Laurent and they were not the same names found in the 1881 census. Interestingly, Etienne Delaronde Jr., listed as a farmer in Saint-Laurent in 1891, was residing with his Lake Manitoba-born wife, Caroline Carrière, at Duck Bay at the time of the 1881 census. He was listed as a labourer in the earlier census. According to his grandson, Etienne Delaronde Jr., he worked for several years on barges hauling freight for the Hudson's Bay Company on Lakes Winnipeg, Manitoba, and Winnipegosis. After leaving the freighting business he operated a ranch at Mary Hill, west of Lundar.[62]

By 1891, Etienne Delaronde Jr. had moved to an area situated 10 kms east of the actual Saint-Laurent river lots commonly called *Coteau de roche*. There he acquired some Aberdeen Angus cattle "direct from Scotland" and started farming in earnest.[63] His nephew and niece, Alexandre (age 24) and Octavie, were boarders at the widow Elise Chartrand's house.[64] Alexandre was a law student, son of Etienne Jr., and a protégé of the Saint-Laurent clergy. Father Camper writes of him: "De son coté, le jeune Alexandre Delaronde continue à être bon garçon et se prépare avec ardeur pour entrer au collège et faire honneur au lac Manitoba."[65] Two Delaronde widows are also listed as heads of family. The first was Marie Anne Desrosiers (age 37), widow of Jean-Baptiste Laronde. Her unmarried son William (age 19) was listed as a farmer. The second widow was Margaret Sinclair (age 48), wife of Paul Delaronde. Her son was also named William (age 16) and he worked as a salaried farm hand.

Etienne Delaronde's brother-in-law, Louis Carrière, had died by the 1891 census. His wife, Julie Marchand, was listed in 1891 as a widowed head of family who took in boarders.[66] Louis Carrière's nephew, Salomon,[67] with his wife Marie MacMillan, is listed as a farmer in 1891. With them lived their unmarried sons, Napoleon (age 29), Alfred (age 25), Ives (age 23), William (age 21), and Henry (age 18). All five are described as literate farm labourers.

Pierre Boyer, the successful claimant to Lot 24 (patented in 1878), had died in July 1880. His widow, Genevieve Martin, with the help of her two sons, still occupied and worked the family property. Elzear (age 24) and Alexandre Boyer (age 22) are listed as literate farmers. The older son, Damase, was a literate farmer and wage earner in his own right. He was married to Philomène, the daughter of Pierre Chartrand and Marie Pangman. All three Boyer sons had come up with their parents from Saint-François-Xavier during the 1868 famine.

The Boyers are a good example of a family establishing a degree of economic affluence and becoming "white." One of the sons of Elzear Boyer, when interviewed in 1987, stated categorically that his father and paternal grandparents were French Canadians from Chicoutimi, Québec. His mother was Marie Anne Delaronde, the daughter of well-to-do Etienne Delaronde Jr. In fact, the narrator's paternal grandparents, Pierre and Geneviève (Martin) Boyer, had declared themselves to be Métis in the 1870 census. Pierre Boyer Jr. was the son of *voyageur* Pierre Boyer Sr., and the *métisse* Marguerite Bonneau. Genevieve Martin's father had been a French Canadian, Abraham Martin, married to a Métis woman from the North-West,

Euphresine Gariépy. However, Elzear Boyer's son, in the course of the interview, stated that he "still" did not admit to being Métis though he noted that his mother's family had been "pretty mixed." In the course of the interview, the respondent's wife added that the "old grandmother," Marie Anne Delaronde, had not wanted her children to mix with those *she* considered to be Métis, and that the "very Métis" families of Fort Rouge would not have considered the Boyers to be "Métis."[68]

The only Goulet family listed in 1891 was that of Pierre Goulet. He was an illiterate hunter and fisherman. His granddaughter, in a 1987 interview, stated that Pierre Goulet and his wife spoke Cree and Saulteaux to each other. Pierre Goulet's wife, Rosalie Goulet, made mittens and moccasins out of moose skins.[69]

The Nabase *dit* Lecris[70] had three heads of family listed in 1891. None was the hunting head of family James Nabase (born 1837, Baie Saint-Paul), the husband of Suzanne Hallet, who was listed in 1881 as being in Saint-Laurent. His brother Louis and wife Marie (Bousquet) Nabase, listed in the 1870 census, appear once more in 1891. Louis Nabase declared himself to be a literate farmer. One of his sons, Pierre (born 1856), married to Marie Richard, worked as a farm labourer. The other brother named Roger[71] worked as a hunter and fisherman.

Aside from families whose members had moved into Saint-Laurent prior to 1870 or during the decade immediately following Manitoba's creation, other Métis families were congregating at Saint-Laurent in the 1880s and early 1890s. Many bought land from the older residents or took up homesteading in nearby areas, such as the previously mentioned *Coteau de roche*. Some families came from the northern part of the lake and from Lake Winnipegosis. For example, Charles and Caroline Monkman, who were listed in 1881 as farming on the shores of Lake Winnipegosis, were in the Saint-Laurent area in 1891. There was also the family of John and Mary Campbell, who arrived from Manitoba House in the early 1880s.[72] Both Charles Monkman and John Campbell were listed as farmers in 1891. However, the immigrants from the north were always a minority of the new arrivals to the area.

The majority of new families came from the more southerly settlements.[73] One family, Alfred and Angélique (née Chartrand of Saint-Laurent) Klyne may have resided in the Lake Winnipegosis area,[74] but Alfred Klyne, a carpenter,[75] came from the southern parish of Sainte-Agathe. There were Eugene and Sarah Allard from Saint-François Xavier, who were described as farmers residing in Saint-Laurent in 1891. (Jean) Baptiste and Marie Anne Beauchamp, also from Saint-François Xavier, were farmers in the parish in 1891. Two brothers, Daniel and Alexandre Coutu,[76] along with their wives and children, also settled to farm in Saint-Laurent. Alexandre Coutu eventually owned a hotel in Saint-Laurent. Another Métis from a prominent Red River (Saint-Norbert) family, Joseph Hamelin Sr., would settle in Saint-Laurent with his wife Julia Laurence. He dealt in groceries and hardware and ran a store[77] with the help of his son, Joseph Jr. This Joseph Hamelin in 1894 married Antoinette Lachance, daughter of the above-mentioned Québec cheese-making and farming family of Sigfroid and Sophie Lachance.[78] Another newcomer, Baptiste Lagimodière, declared himself to be a farmer in 1891.

A new Métis family to come up from the southern parishes was that of Charles

A photograph of the CNR train arriving in Saint-Laurent, 1920.

Lambert of the parish of Saint-Norbert, with his wife, Marie Laurence.[79] She was the sister of Julia Laurence, wife of the above-mentioned merchant Joseph Hamelin.[80] Charles Lambert was listed in 1891 as a farm labourer but, according to his grand-daughter (interviewed in 1984), by the time she was a young child in the first decade of the 20th century, he owned seven or eight milk cows. By the second decade of the twentieth century he was shipping his cream by train[81] to Winnipeg.[82] This was a family that, by 1910, had successfully integrated into the farming element of Lake Manitoba. Charles's son, Arcade, husband of Catherine Lavallée, had approximately 22 milk cows and they farmed 62 acres. His children all went to school for several years. One of Charles Lambert's granddaughters, in the 1984 interview, stated categorically that she was not Métis and did not want to be identified as such: "c'est pas beau être Métis."[83] This even though she noted that her Lavallée grandparents had spoken Saulteaux with greater facility than French: "tous des parleurs de saulteaux les Lavallée." She added that her (Lavallée) mother never spoke a word of Saulteaux to the children and that the Lamberts had no relatives in Saint-Laurent's fringe settlement of Fort Rouge.

If we assume the data in the 1891 census to be largely correct, a trend can be detected. The early Lake Manitoba families, those who had settled the area prior to 1868, even if they held patent to a piece of land, were still actively pursuing the same activities they had prior to 1870: hunting, trapping, fishing, and to a certain extent, trading. This group is probably much larger than indicated by the census, since the *hivernant* category is missing.[84] If we look at the returns for families arriving at Saint-Laurent after 1868 (post-famine), and especially after 1880, they show an increasing concern for farming or wage labour and commercial activities. Of course there are exceptions—the majority of the lakeshore population would engage in fishing and some hunting, whatever their origins. The variation between the different Métis groups (the "founding families," those arriving in the late 1860s, fleeing the famine, and those arriving after 1870)[85] is what they perceived as their primary economic activity. The post-1880 families[86] were certainly agriculturally minded (coupled to fishing), and they had enough capital to buy sections of river lots or land held by speculators in nearby sections.[87] It would have been interesting to find the receipt books from the different butter and cheese factories to see who was in a position to sell cream and in what quantity. One suspects that the majority of cream would have been from families of the post-1870 migration, with the previously noted exceptions. Again, what should be emphasised is the absence of a large contingent of *hivernants* in the censuses discussed.

Between 1891 and 1914, the pressures brought to bear on the lakeshore Métis population would increase. Incoming Breton migrants, with their negative perception of "traditional" North-West lifestyles, and a changing economic climate, would further fragment the old Saint-Laurent population. Divergent groups would emerge between 1891 and 1914, but, contrary to popular perception, they would have a class rather than an ethnic basis. Many families who in 1914 labelled themselves "French Canadian" or "Indian" had, 30 years before, been labelled Métis. In the next chapter the tendencies of persistence or assimilation, and the forces that produced them, will be examined for the years from 1891 to 1914.

CHAPTER 5

The Fragmentation of a "Métis" Community, 1891–1901

B ETWEEN 1891 AND THE TURN OF THE CENTURY the population of Saint-Laurent rose *officially* from about 600 to 769 (623 described as "Métis," 49 as "French," 88 as "English," and two "others").[1] The increase appears to be both natural and from immigration. Though no large influx of migrants is noted in the clerical correspondence, the 1901 Census does note the arrival of "new" families—some Métis, but others arriving from Eastern Canada, France, Ireland and Scotland. The economic pursuits of the Saint-Laurent residents continued to be a combination of traditional lakeshore activities (hunting and fishing) and farming pursuits. The overall number of full-time hunter-fishermen may have declined slightly in those years as a new fish house was erected just north of Saint-Laurent, in the municipality of Posen, and several families who depended on fishing for a living relocated there.[2] Some may also have relocated permanently to the *Rivière du Cygne* area or the Narrows, as fish buyers became more willing to go where people were fishing.

In fact, only one head of household was listed as being a fisherman. The literate, English-speaking Métis William Isbister (age 36), with his wife Catherine and three children, are listed as making $200 a year from fishing and $200 from "extra earnings." However the same caveat noted for the previous censuses still exits in 1901. This last census was conducted in Saint-Laurent during the last half of the month of April. This was a month when the ice on the lakes would be breaking, and was a time usually devoted to muskrat hunting.

Certainly, taken at face value, the 1901 census gives the impression that the Saint-Laurent parish had become a very polarized community. William Logan, the census taker, counted 124 households during his stay in Saint-Laurent from April 11 to April 30. On paper the occupational divisions are sharp. Of the 156 individuals[3] declaring an occupation, none declared dual pursuits. This is unlike all previous censuses, where descriptions with combinations such as "hunter & fisherman" were found. In order of frequency, 52 respondents declared themselves to be "hunters," 47 were "farmers," 14 were "ranchers," nine were "servants" or "farm hands," six were "labourers," five were "carpenters," five were "peddlers/merchants," four were "clerks," three were "teachers," two were "butchers," one was a "blacksmith," one was a "notary" (from France), one was a fisherman, and one was a salaried cheese maker. Interestingly, there appears to be an "ethnic overlap" to the occupation declared. Logan defined all 52 hunters as "Cree or Chippewa HalfBreeds" (i.e., Métis). A majority of servants, farm hands and labourers are also seen as Métis. Only 26 Métis heads of family (or their adult children) would declare themselves to be ranchers or farmers out of a total of 61 respondents for these two categories combined.

The importance of agriculture in the municipality of Saint-Laurent increased slightly between 1891 and 1901, as can be seen in the table on the following page.

In fact, the number of cattle may have been greater in 1895 than in either 1891 or 1901. In the spring of 1895, for example, *Le Métis* noted that:

> M. le comte de Leusse établit une fromagerie qui commencera à fonctionner dans les premiers jours de mai. Déjà M. F. Rey en montait une avec plein succès. Pour mémoire je cite celle de M.

Agricultural Statistics, Saint-Laurent Municipality, 1901					
Township	Acres Cultivated	Horses	Cattle	Sheep	Pigs
16-2W		26	200	2	16
16-4W		23	135	8	45
Saint-Laurent	381	155	458	10	76
17-4W	84	192	129	19	15
Oak Point	45	36	135	8	11

Saint-Laurent Municipality, Tax Assessment Roll: 1901. Taken from J.M. Richtik,
Historical Geography of the Interlake Area of Manitoba From 1871 to 1921, 170
(Table 14).

> Trudel, connue depuis quelques années et fort appréciée. M. E.
> Trudel dirigera celle de M. le comte de Leusse. Une autre encore
> doit s'organiser pour le commencement de la saison chez Mme
> Viel.[4]

> *The Count of Leusse has established a cheese-making operation that will be
> starting up in the beginning of May. Already, Mr. F. Rey is operating a
> successful one. I remind you of Mr. Trudel's that has been functioning for
> a few years and is highly appreciated. Mr. E. Trudel will be in charge of the
> one owned by the Count of Leusse. Another cheese factory is to be organised
> for the beginning of the season at the home of Mrs. Viel.*

Six weeks later *Le Métis* added that "M.M. Coutu établissent une fromagerie; ce qui
portent à six le nombre des établissements [à Saint-Laurent]."[5] The Coutu family
is the only case of a post-1880 "Métis" family having the capital to start such an
enterprise. By the turn of the century the ever-growing railway system had resulted
in the consolidation of cheese and butter factories in larger centres, such as
Winnipeg, and the closing down of many small rural factories.

In 1901 Saint-Laurent continued to experience the economic restructuring that
had resulted, since the 1860s, in growing social, economic and "racial" fragmenta-
tion.[6] Saint-Laurent's economic development was still based on the production of
staples such as fish, cream, and furs. In many ways, its economy strongly resembled
that of the more northern communities on Lake Winnipegosis with which it had
familial and business ties.[7] The village was linked to an international market
through its production of pelts and fish. But, unlike the northern settlements, it
was also tied to the provincial economy through the selling of cream to local cheese
or butter factories or directly to Winnipeg.[8] It was this agricultural "provincial" link
that was crucial in crystallising socio-economic differences in Saint-Laurent.

As discussed in the previous chapters, the Saint-Laurent "farming" segment was
composed largely of representatives of four categories of people. First there were
the members of two of the four founding clans. Second, there were families that
took refuge in Saint-Laurent during the 1867–68 famine. Third, most of the families arriving in Saint-Laurent from the more southerly parishes in the 1880s and
1890s engaged in some form of agriculture. Fourth, a few moneyed European and
Québécois families came specifically to Saint-Laurent to farm.

As the 1901 census returns indicate, the four founding clans continued the trend noted in previous decades. No Pangman or Sayer representatives were present in Saint-Laurent in April 1901. Of the 11 resident Lavallée households, all were listed as having a hunter as head of family. In fact, they occupied no other economic category. The Chartrands in Saint-Laurent and elsewhere continued a trend towards a much more diverse economic base. If we look at Saint-Laurent and its three satellite communities of Oak Point, Pine Creek (future Camperville) and Winnipegosis (Duck Bay), only three heads of household were listed as hunters. Eleven Chartrand men were fishermen, mostly working out of Pine Creek. Six declared a variety of occupations from cheese maker[9] to merchant,[10] while three were farmers and one was a rancher. Obviously those family members opting to remain in Saint-Laurent were involving themselves in a variety of occupations.

Several Métis families that arrived in the area from 1868 onward, some after 1891, are represented in the non-"hunting & menial occupations" categories. Only Cuthbert Ducharme, son of Jean-Baptiste Ducharme, was listed as farming in the parish. His father had been listed as the only Ducharme farmer in the 1891 census. The three Richard heads of family residing in Saint-Laurent declared their occupation to be hunting. Both in 1881 and in 1891 several Richard men had declared themselves to be carpenters. This would not be the case in 1901. Three Desjarlais families were listed, each with a head of family holding a different occupation. Antoine Desjarlais, married to Marie Chartrand and father to eight children, was described as a carpenter. Ten years prior Antoine had been a farm labourer. His older son, Antoine Desjarlais Jr., married to "Esther," was listed as a general servant making $60 a year. Another son, François Desjarlais, was described as a hunter. Seven Chaboyer households were listed in the 1901 census. This is one clan that appears not to have chosen or been able to make the transition to a farming life. All, with the exception of ranch hand Gaspar, were listed as hunters. Nabase, or Nabez *dit* Lecris, is another family, like the Chaboyers, which was clearly defined as a hunting family by 1901. The three adult Nabez men, two of whom were married, were listed as hunters. Their father, Louis Nabez, had declared himself a farmer but in 1901 he was no longer found in the parish. Only the families of Roger and Patrice Nabez remained by the 1910 parish survey.[11]

Salomon and Marie (née MacMillan) Carrière were still farming in 1901. Living with them were six of their children 17 years of age and older. All could read and write in French and speak English. None were listed as working for wages. With them lived Salomon's widowed mother, Suzanne Ducharme (age 97), wife of Alexis Carrière.

Only one Boyer was listed in the 1901 census—Elzéar, son of Pierre Boyer and Genevieve Martin. Both he and his two brothers were listed as literate farmers in 1891. By 1901 Elzear Boyer was still a farmer, married to Marie Anne Delaronde, daughter of Etienne and Helen (Monkman) Delaronde. They had two children— Marie (age one year) and Alvina (age three months). Damase Boyer (married to Philomène Chartrand) and Alexandre Boyer (married to Claire Boivin) were not present in the spring of 1901. Alexandre had married in Saint-François Xavier in

1901 Census Province of Manitoba

Pine Creek

Heads of Household	Occupation	People in Household	School Age Children	Attending School	Read and Write	Speak English Language	Speak French Language	Mother Tongue	Racial Origin
CHARTRAND									
Pierre (II)	fisherman	9	6	0	1	2	4	Ojibway	Amerindian
Gaspard (II)	fisherman	4	0	0	0	0	4	Ojibway	Amerindian
François (II)	fisherman	4	2	0	0	1	4	Ojibway	Amerindian
William (II)	fisherman	9	6	0	3	4	8	Ojibway	Amerindian
Michel (II) *	carter	8	0	0	0	2	2	Ojibway	Amerindian
Louis (II)	fishermen	2	0	0	0	4	4	Ojibway	Amerindian
Louison (III)	fisherman	3	0	0	0	2	2	Ojibway	Amerindian
Alexandre (III)	fisherman	10	5	0	0	1	2	Ojibway	Amerindian
Moïse (III)	fisherman	8	5	0	0	1	0	Ojibway	Amerindian
Sophie (widow of **MICHEL I**)	1 fisherman	6	1	0	1	2	2	Ojibway	Amerindian
Alexandre (II)	fisherman	7	3	0	0	1	1	Cree	Amerindian
Elzéar (II)	fisherman	7	5	0	1	1	1	Ojibway	Amerindian
Totals		77	33	0	6	21	34		

* Michel appears twice in the 1901 census; also appears in Winnipegosis with same family.

Oak Point

Heads of Household	Occupation	People in Household	School Age Children	Attending School	Read and Write	Speak English Language	Speak French Language	Mother Tongue	Racial Origin
Paul (II)	rancher	6	3	2	3	5	6	French	Cree
Hermas (III)	hunter	7	4	3	3	4	5	Chippewa	Chippewa
Norbert (II)	hunter	12	6	3	5	8	8	French	Cree
Totals		25	13	8	11	17	19		

1901 Census Province of Manitoba

Winnipegosis

Heads of Household	Occupation	People in Household	School Age Children	Attending School	Read and Write	Speak English Language	Speak French Language	Mother Tongue	Racial Origin
CHARTRAND									
JOSEPH (II)	?	8	4	0	0	6	6	French	French Breed
MICHEL (II)	farmer	9	5	1	4	8	8	French	?
Totals		**17**	**9**	**1**	**4**	**14**	**14**		

Saint-Laurent

Heads of Household	Occupation	People in Household	School Age Children	Attending School	Read and Write	Speak English Language	Speak French Language	Mother Tongue	Racial Origin
Antoine (II)	1-hunter 1- farm hand	3	0	0	1	1	3	Chippewa	Chippewa
Patrice (III)	farmer	6	3	2	4	2	4	Chippewa	Chippewa
Joseph (III)	general servant	3	0	0	1	0	2	Chippewa	Chippewa
Marie-Louise (widow of Magloire II)	seamstress	5	3	3	4	3	4	French	Cree
Baptiste (II)	farmer	7	2	2	5	4	5	French	Cree
Hermas (II)	municipal clerk	7	3	2	4	4	6	French	Cree
Napoléon (II)	cheese maker	2	0	0	1	1	2	French	Cree
Michel (II)	merchant	8	4	2	5	2	7	Cree	Chippewa
Totals		**41**	**15**	**11**	**25**	**17**	**33**		

1901 Census Province of Manitoba

Pine Creek

Heads of Household	Occupation	Number People in household	School Age Children	Attending School	Read and Write	Speak English Language	Speak French Language	Mother tongue	racial origin
PANGMAN									
PIERRE (I)	fisherman	7	4	0	0	1	1	Ojibway	Amerindian
MICHEL (I)	fisherman	3	0	0	0	0	1	Ojibway	Amerindian
Napoléon (II)	millhand	2	0	0	2	2	2	Ojibway	Amerindian
Jean (II)	fisherman	5	1	0	2	3	3	Ojibway	Amerindian
PATRICE (I)	millhand	4	1	0	0	2	2	Ojibway	Amerindian
Totals		**21**	**6**	**0**	**4**	**8**	**9**		

Saint-Laurent

Heads of Household	Occupation	Number People in household	School Age Children	Attending School	Read and Write	Speak English Language	Speak French Language	Mother tongue	racial origin
LAVALLÉE									
ANTOINE (I)	hunter	7	2	1	6	1	4	Cree	Cree
Antoine (II)	hunter	4	0	0	0	1	3	french	Cree
Patrice (II)	hunter	2	0	0	1	1	2	Cree	Cree
Michel (I)	hunter	10	4	3	6	3	9	Cree	Cree
Joseph (II)	hunter	2	0	0	1	1	2	Cree	Cree
JOSEPH (II)	hunter	5	0	0	3	1	3	Cree	Cree
Joseph Michel (II)	hunter	3	6	3	2	1	7	Cree	Cree
Pierre (II)	hunter	10	4	3	4	2	7	Cree	Cree
John (II)	hunter	10	5	4	5	4	3	Cree	Cree
ANDRE (I)	hunter	8	2	0	7	1	1	Cree	Cree
André (w) (II)	hunter	3	2	0	0	1	1	Cree	Cree
Baptiste (w) (II)	hunter	2	1	0	1	1	—	Cree	Cree
Totals		**66**	**22**	**13**	**32**	**17**	**40**		

1901 Census Province of Manitoba

	Number of Households	Number in Household	Children School age	school Attending	Read	Write	Language Speak English	Language Speak French
Pine Creek								
Chartrand	12	77	33	0	6		21	34
Lavallée	0	0	0	0	0		0	0
Pangman	5	21	6	0	4		8	9
Sayer	0	0	0	0	0		0	0
Saint-Laurent								
Chartrand	8	41	15	11	25		17	33
Lavallée	11	66	22	13	32		8	44
Pangman	0	0	0	0	0		0	0
Sayer	0	0	0	0	0		0	0
Oak Point								
Chartrand		25	13	8	11		17	19
Lavallée		0	0	0	0		0	0
Pangman		0	0	0	0		0	0
Sayer		0	0	0	0		0	0
Winnipegosis								
Chartrand		17	9	1	4		14	14
Lavallée		0	0	0	0		0	0
Pangman		0	0	0	0		0	0
Sayer		0	0	0	0		0	0

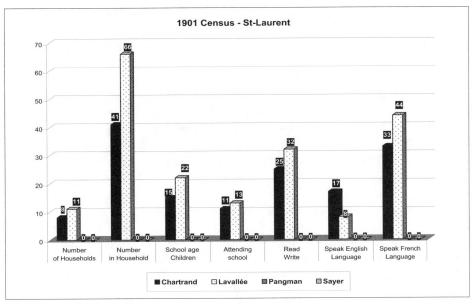

1901 Census - St-Laurent

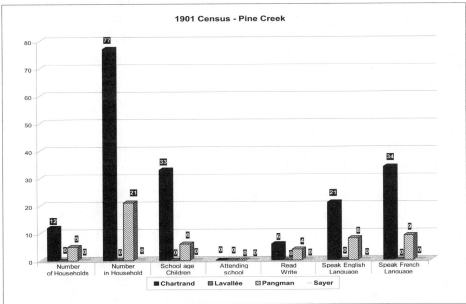

1901 Census - Pine Creek

1894 and had buried a son there in April 1900. He may have opted to move back to his place of birth in the previous decade.

Looking at the northern families, no Monkmans were present in 1901, but two Campbell heads of family were listed in the census. John Campbell (age 26, b. Manitoba House) was married to "Madeleine." With them lived their three children and a youth also named John Campbell (age 15), brother to the first John. In the parish there also resided their uncle Charles Campbell (age 37), with his wife Marie Rose Tchi-an and their six children aged 2 to 16. Like several of the Chaboyers and Nabez, unschooled and illiterate, they declared their maternal language to be Cree but stated their capacity to speak both French and English. Both Campbells declared their occupation to be hunting.

Alfred Klyne (age 31), married to Angelique Chartrand[12] (age 32), was listed as a labourer. Ten years previously he had been described as a carpenter. They had six children, the oldest age 10, and declared their annual income to be $140 with $60 in "extra income." They are the only Klyne household in Saint-Laurent.

The two Saint-François Xavier families which had moved to the settlement in the 1880s were still present in 1901. Sarah Allard, widow of Eugene Allard, ran the only Allard household in Saint-Laurent. She was the only woman listed as a woman farming head of family. She had five children living with her ages 4 to 18. The Beauchamp clan had four families residing in Saint-Laurent at the beginning of the 20th century. The eldest, Jean-Baptiste (age 69), was listed as a labourer. In 1891 he had been described as a farmer. He and his wife, Marie Anne Gunville (age 69), had two adult sons, Gabriel and Joseph, and a four-year-old orphan "William" listed as dependents without declared professions. The other three Beauchamp heads of family, likely older sons, are all described as hunters. All trilingual with Cree as their maternal tongue, only one claims to have reading skills.

By 1901, there were four Coutu brothers residing in Saint-Laurent. The original two brothers—Daniel, married to Marie Chaboyer, and Alexandre, married to Rosalie Chaboyer—were again listed as farmers. Alexandre Coutu was head of an especially large household. His widowed French-Canadian father, Pierre Henri Coutu (age 66), and three younger brothers—Edmond (b. 1886), Charles (b. 1882),[13] and Louis (b. 1885)—were also part of the household. Another resident of the household was Romain Lagimoniere, an 85-year-old French-Canadian patriarch, father-in-law to Pierre Henri Coutu, described in the census as a farmer.[14] Two other Coutu brothers—Victor (age 35), married to Marie Lavallée, and George (age 34), married to Rosalie Cyr—were also considered literate bilingual farmers.

By 1901 only Joseph Hamelin and his wife, Antoinette Lachance, represented those two families in Saint-Laurent. As noted in the preceding chapter, the large Lachance extended family had moved to the Saint-Eustache-Baie Saint-Paul area with their cattle herd after a difficult drought in 1892–93. The couple was considered literate with French as their maternal tongue. Joseph Hamelin also spoke English.

Charles Lambert and Marie Laurence were still a farming family in 1901. An indication of the caution with which the data gleaned from censuses must be treated comes from the life history of Charles Lambert's son, Arcade. As noted previously, he and his wife, Catherine Lavallée, would become a successful farming household by the end of their lives. But, as a young man in 1901, Arcade Lambert was considered just another illiterate hunter in the census rolls.

Beginning in 1906, the farming and fishing families were augmented by the arrival of French immigrants brought in directly from Brittany (France) to farm and fish in Saint-Laurent. To the large French contingent can be added a few French-Canadian families brought in by Father Peran of the Oblates in an effort to "whiten," "frenchify," and settle Saint-Laurent. The Oblates wished to transform the parish into a fully agricultural settlement more in keeping with the clergy's idea of a proper Catholic settlement.[15] By the end of the 19th century it was the declared intention of the Oblate order, working in the vicariate of Saint-Boniface, to encourage French-Canadian or French-European migration into Manitoba in the hopes of establishing a firm, rural Catholic bastion. Not much hope was placed on the success of sedentarising Manitoba's Métis and Indian population. The explanation for the perceived lack of success in the Oblates' effort at Native farming was clearly considered to be biological:

> L'œuvre des Missions sauvages est très belle, mais, après tout, l'avenir n'est point à ces races affaiblies, il appartient aux races européennes, qui s'établissent partout dans nos plaines fertiles. Il n'est pas moins glorieux et méritoire de fonder des royaumes nouveaux et d'établir, sur des bases solides le royaume de Jésus Christ dans le nouveau monde.[16]

> *The work done by the Native missions is laudable but, after all, the future does not belong to these weakened races. It belongs to those European races that are settling on our fertile plains. It is no less glorious and meritorious to create new kingdoms and to establish, on solid bases, the kingdom of God in the new world.*

About 126 Bretons (men, women and children) settled in Saint-Laurent. The November 1910 parish census notes the presence of 21 immigrant French families.[17] The writers of the time noted that the immigrants all came with some capital. Also, none chose to try their hand at homesteading, preferring instead to purchase land which suited them: "aucun ne prit de homestead; tous préfèrent acheter des terrains à leur goût et être de suite entièrement maître chez eux."[18] Most had been farmers in their homeland and in Saint-Laurent they concentrated their efforts on gardening, dairy farming and, eventually with great success, ice fishing. Some Bretons also undertook commercial and wage labour activities. For example, two Breton heads of family bought a haypress in 1911 and the following year were successfully buying up local hay and selling it at a profit to more southerly farmers. Another specialised in the clearing of forested areas for farming: "[il] trouve que cela paie largement, d'autant plus que ce travail extra n'empêche pas sa femme et ses enfants de faire marcher la ferme."[19] Many younger sons would work for wages on neighbouring farms during the summer months. They would return in autumn to Saint-Laurent where their summer wages would be invested in the family farm, a tradition that did not seem prevalent among the Métis population. By 1911 all the Breton senior heads of family were proprietors of fairly well-equipped farms: "bien montée et d'une importance proportionelle aux fonds dont ils disposaient à leur arrivée."[20] To this group can be added three Irish Catholic families totalling 27 individuals,[21] one adult male of Belgian descent, and two French-Canadian families (14 people).

While Saint-Laurent was experiencing an influx of "moneyed" settlers, many of the old settlers of Oak Point were leaving that small settlement[22] to be replaced by Icelandic fishermen.[23] The arrival of European settlers and their apparent success hardened the attitude of lay and church authorities[24] towards the hunting and gathering element of the population. In published and private correspondence, writers began to refer to the hunting and gathering group as "Indians," perhaps increasingly unwilling to accept that people with French Catholic ancestors would lead such a life and be so reluctant to speak any other language but Cree or Saulteaux. As early as 1896 Father Camper would write to Mgr. Langevin, making no mention of "Métis":

> Le catéchisme de la première communion a commencé cette semaine. C'est une besogne d'un mois ou d'un mois et demi. Le père Gascon et le père Dorais l'ont entrepris. Le premier ce charge des Français, le second des Anglais et des Sauteux.[25]

> *The catechism for the first communion has begun this week. It is a task that will last a month or a month and a half. Father Gascon and Father Dorais have undertaken the task. The first is in charge of the French, the second of the English and Saulteaux.*

In a letter published in 1907, Father L. Gladu, OMI, would describe Saint-Laurent's population in the following startling terms: "La paroisse de Saint-Laurent est composée de quatre populations de langues diverses: des Bretons, des Canadiens français, des Irlandais, et des sauvages Sauteux."[26]

The clerical distancing from, and disapproval of, old Métis families who did not conform to western (European) ideas of proper behaviour was shared by the recent French-Canadian and Breton immigrants:

> Il est logique que cet état de décomposition se traduise par l'isolement d'une grande partie de la société métisse dans les provinces de l'Ouest. *On ne saurait attendre d'éléments réduits à ce degré de déchéance qu'ils obtiennent, du moins en nombre appréciable, un droit d'accès à la société blanche.* Ou bien, lorsque les unions s'accomplissent, elles risquent fort de se faire entre éléments de même niveau, et de demeurer sans profit pour les métis. L'isolement se manifeste déjà dans les groupes que nous avons observés autour des lacs Winnipeg et Manitoba, dont la décadence est pourtant moins prononcée. *A Saint-Laurent, Français et Canadien s'unissent dans un égal mépris du groupe de couleur. Leur hostilité s'y exprime en paroles malveillantes, presque haineuses, surtout de la part des familles françaises récemment introduites par les Pères Oblats:* la conduite de celles-ci, faite de travail et d'abnégation, ne saurait s'harmoniser avec les habitudes de vie des Métis… Et il existe nous l'avons vu, parmi les Métis des familles assez évoluées pour ne pas encourir sans injustice, l'hostilité systématique des Blancs. Mais les alliances qui s'opèrent entre les uns et les autres sont mal vues de ces

derniers. Non seulement elles ne dissipent points leurs préventions, mais elles paraissent les aggraver. C'est précisément des Canadiens dont les familles comptent une ou plusieurs unions de cette nature qu'émanent les critiques les plus sévères, *comme s'ils éprouvaient une vive humiliation d'avoir à admettre parmi eux des représentants de ce groupe inférieur.*[27]

It is only logical that this state of decomposition translates itself into the isolation of the greater part of the western Métis population. We cannot expect that elements reduced to such a level of decadence be admitted in any great number into white society. If any unions do occur they risk being between elements of the same social level and will be of no profit to the Métis. Isolation is noticed in the groups we have observed on the shores of Lakes Winnipeg and Manitoba, even though the level of decadence is less pronounced there. In Saint-Laurent, French and "Canadiens" come together to express their disdain for the coloured group. Their hostility expresses itself in hostile, nearly hateful words, especially coming from the French families recently introduced by the Oblate Fathers. The life of these French families is defined by work and sacrifice and cannot harmonise itself with the life habits of the Métis. As we have seen, there do exist among the Métis group families evolved enough not to deserve the systematic hostility of the whites. But when [marital] alliances occur between these two groups they do nothing to dissipate their [white] concerns. In fact, these alliances seem to increase the levels of worry. It is within the "Canadien" group whose families have known one or several of these unions that criticism is at its worst. It is as if they [the Canadiens] feel an intense humiliation at having to accept amongst themselves representatives of this inferior group.

By 1910 the "farming" segment of Saint-Laurent was composed largely of recently arrived French immigrants, but it also included families of "Métis" descent which were successfully integrated into the agrarian economy.[28] They, unlike families more fully tied to an international economy by their greater dependence on fishing and trapping, were always assured of a steady market for their products between 1881 and 1919.[29] During economic slowdowns, as in the mid-1890s and just prior to World War I, dairy farmers did suffer a decline in their incomes. However, the downward trend was not as pronounced as that experienced by other primary producers.[30]

Between 1900 and 1945, most residents of Saint-Laurent were fishing commercially to some degree. The arrival of the railway in 1904 tied producers more fully to international markets, especially Chicago.[31] The link to international capitalism was a mixed blessing since, by pushing up demand and production, it threatened to deplete fish stocks. As early as 1884 Father Camper expressed concern at the poor catches fishermen were getting. He feared some families might be facing famine (being unable to get supplies and credit at a store): "La pêche avec la chasse aux lièvres sont à peu près leurs seuls moyens de vivre dans l'hiver ces dernières années."[32] Again, in 1890, the Department of Indian affairs had noted:

The lower portion of Lake Winnipeg and portions of Lake Manitoba have ceased to be good fishing grounds after having been operated upon by large fishing establishments for a comparatively short period of time.[33]

This last comment also reveals the direct competition individual fishermen were facing from large companies. Independent fishermen in Saint-Laurent had difficulty absorbing the loss of property and lives that occurred frequently through storms and treacherous ice conditions. For example, one respondent related to the Chartrand clan noted that, in one stormy night, he lost his whole "outfit" of 102 nets. He had gone out too early in the season to lay his nets and, as a result of a windstorm, the ice had broken up on the lake. He had acquired the initial capital necessary to purchase his fishing equipment by working for a Breton farmer, cutting hay for $15 a month. This fisherman had no land to fall back on.[34]

The problems plaguing small Saint-Laurent fishing families between 1900 and 1945 were similar to those faced by independent farmers the world over. Hundreds of commodity producers sold to a handful of companies that often cooperated and reinvested most of the profits outside of the Lake Manitoba and Lake Winnipegosis regions. As the Rothney-Watson report notes:

> Only 4 frozen fish companies (largely controlled by American capital) operated in Manitoba and by the 1930s they were cooperating to reduce competition. The individual producers were largely helpless in advocating for better prices and efforts at organizing largely failed due to difficulties of sustaining collective mass solidarity within the confines of a capitalist market ... and no permanent and mutual group spirit emerges from an organization based on motives of diversity, individualism and self-interest.[35]

Intensified competition during favourable market periods and cyclical slumps in prices due to an unstable international economy meant a precarious existence for those of the Saint-Laurent fishermen who were heavily dependent on food staples that had to be purchased with cash or credit at a store. An example of fluctuating prices is the 1914–15 slump in demand. By early February prices were cut by 50% from the previous winter, and by the end of the month buyers had stopped buying altogether.[36] This spelled disaster for fishermen who had gone into debt to get onto the ice. Prices would continue to fluctuate after World War I. For example, by 1920–21 the prices given for fish were the highest in living memory[37] and most fishermen were able to clear a profit, making the "Métis" villagers' continued reluctance to pay church dues a mystery to the religious authorities. Prosperity was not to last. In the 1930s, prices once again plummeted:

> Market conditions have changed considerably in the last few years and what was once an extensive and favourable market cannot now absorb present production at any price and indeed can only take care of a fraction of the whole production at any price which will net the fishermen even a small profit.[38]

Fishermen were faced with seasonal debts (getting outfitted, credit during a bad year, unexpected low prices) that often left little room for capital accumulation.[39] Moreover, though prices tended to rise there is little evidence that fishermen's buying power increased proportionately. Profits did not "trickle" down to primary producers.[40] For some of the more common species of fish, such as whitefish, prices offered to the fishermen would remain low for decades.[41]

As previously stated, Saint-Laurent fishermen never really formed a distinct social and economic (or "racial") grouping. Farmers, hunters and gatherers, and trappers all participated in the winter fishing industry. What distinguished the participants from each other was the *importance* of fishing in the family budget, the scale on which it was undertaken, and the other staple-producing activities linked to it. The families considered *notable*, that is, families that had attained a certain degree of material well-being and social acceptability, were combining fishing with dairy farming.[42] The revenues derived from these activities must have been considerable since the church authorities in 1905 expected them to pay the greatest amount of tithes, $10 a year. Only 35 families out of a total of nearly 200 were considered well-to-do by the Oblates.[43]

These farmer-fisherman families could put up to 200 nets under the ice and their "outfits" were comprised of at least one team of horses (later Bombardiers) and some hired hands. If the season was good they were able to clear a substantial profit, and reinvest in other activities.[44] If the catch or the market was poor, they could count on income from cream or hay sales to recoup their losses, honour their debts (at least partially), and pay their Freemen Métis hired hands. Produce from their gardens and their cattle lessened their dependence on merchants for basic foodstuffs. Though there were differences in herd size, numbers of fish nets put out, degree of land and capital controlled and, last but not least, level of help (financial or other) received from religious authorities,[45] all could weather several bad fishing seasons without being beggared.

At the other end of the socio-economic scale were the "Fort-Rouge" residents, most of whom also engaged in fishing. As stated in Chapter 3, Fort Rouge was an impoverished fringe area of Saint-Laurent situated, literally, on the other side of the train tracks from the main mission area and containing, at its most populous, a few dozen households. Several of the heads of family listed as hunters in 1881 and 1891 resided there. Several older Manitoba villages had such small communities on their outskirts. These seem to have been given distinct names to emphasise their separateness.[46]

Respondents defined Fort Rouge as somehow more traditional. The fishing-farming respondents, in the course of interviews, considered the Fort Rouge residents to be "closer" in appearance and custom to the Indians. Most, during the first half of the 20th century, still spoke Cree or Saulteaux to each other and the women still wore the traditional black shawl and smoked corn pipes.[47] Though the origins of Fort Rouge are nebulous, indications are that descendants of the families listed as indigent in the 1867–68 famine, and hunting-and-gathering families who had moved into the settlement in the 1880s and 1890s, formed a majority of

Changing times: many of the Métis in the Saint-Laurent area continued to practice traditional occupations, such as ice fishing. In this photo, taken in the mid-20th century, we see two fishermen, but the traditional team of horses has been replaced by a Bombardier.

its population. After 1880 very little homestead land was available and, unlike families coming from the older southern Métis parishes, these hunter-gatherers did not have the capital necessary to buy land outright. Some of these Fort Rouge families managed to acquire a few cattle that they pastured on "unoccupied" land. According to an old Fort Rouge respondent, cattle could make life quite a bit easier for hunting and fishing families.[48] By the early 20th century property owners were beginning to fence their property and the hay lands behind the river (lake) lots were being homesteaded or claimed and bought for private use. Prior to the fencing, haying appears to have been done largely on a first-come first-served basis. One respondent explained how he had built up a "ranch" where only the house was fenced in. The cattle roamed free. When land began to be fenced, in he realised that even if he sold his herd (74 head), he would still not have enough capital to acquire sufficient property for a viable farming operation.[49]

Well-to-do residents of Saint-Laurent thought of Fort Rouge as a tough place, had few social contacts with its inhabitants, and denied having relatives there.[50] In the clergy's eyes, the Fort Rouge Métis had serious problems when it came to religious or moral obligations and duties.[51] Oblates would deplore their "savage" mentality, their reluctance to obey directives given at the pulpit and their tight-fistedness when it came to paying church dues.[52] At the turn of the century the resident priest repeated a frequent complaint:

> Il y en a toujours qui se plaignent. Ils peuvent tout dépenser pour satisfaire leur vanité, leur orgueil, leur passion, leurs désirs déréglés, pour les plaisirs, pour la boissons, etc... et ils n'ont que des murmures et des plaintes à faire entendre quand on leur demande quelque chose pour le Bon Dieu![53]

> *There are always those who complain. They will do anything to satisfy their vanity, their passion, their uncontrolled desires for pleasures and drinking. But when we ask them something for the good Lord all we hear are murmurs and complaints!*

In their defence, the impoverished villagers would point to the Oblates' prize-winning dairy herd, large land holdings, and stone buildings, and query the necessity for more tithes. Outside funds had established the church's presence in Saint-Laurent, and therefore the Oblates should look elsewhere for money.

What really distinguished Fort Rouge residents from other villagers (aside from their clearly being labelled "Métis") was their serious poverty, which often resulted in hunger.[54] The Fort Rouge Métis did not own land. Some had never participated in the land claims or scrip processes while others had sold their claims early. They did not have the money to build up a dairy farm. They could not (because of the seasonal demands of their subsistence activities) plant large gardens. These Métis were even more sensitive to the vagaries of an international economy than their more established and sedentary neighbours.[55]

Interview data indicate that the activities open to the Fort Rouge settlers condemned them to a life of poverty. In winter they fished on a small scale with the help of dogs and sleighs on the edge of the lakes, and rarely put out more than 20 or 25 nets. What was left after family (and dog) needs were met was sold to the fish companies. Since prices were usually quite low, large quantities needed to be harvested for the fishery to be profitable. Presumably, in a good year some money could be made, since these fishermen had little overhead cost.[56] However a series of bad years could be disastrous and, as Lagassé points out, alternative sources of income came into direct conflict with home gardening, which could have lessened their dependence on store-bought foodstuffs. All in all, the above indicates the existence of the Fort Rouge settlers as a separate economic group at the lowest end of the scale.

Besides fishing, the Fort Rouge Métis engaged in trapping, berry picking, digging seneca root, and frog harvesting, coupled to some form of seasonal wage labour.[57] There are indications that having few earthly possessions could be an advantage in years of hardship. One respondent explained that during a difficult period four (unnamed) Saint-Laurent men left almost unnoticed to fish on Great Slave Lake (NWT) for a few seasons.[58] Some Fort Rouge hunting-and-gathering families were quite willing to relocate themselves for years in an effort to improve returns from their labour. One respondent, born in 1909, remembered her family leaving Saint-Laurent for bush country north of Wabowden and The Pas so that her father could hunt, trap and work as a freighter. In the summer they went up to Nelson House to fish for sturgeon. Activities such as muskrat hunting could be profitable endeavours in years when catches were plentiful and the price was good: "Une seule maison de commerce ici (Saint-Laurent) a expedié 20,000 peaux de rat musqués!"[59] Eventually, the family returned to Saint-Laurent in the 1920s when several of the children were of school age.

Other non-Fort Rouge villagers also participated from time to time in such endeavours but viewed them as sources of *supplementary* income to be undertaken when time permitted.[60] For the Fort Rouge Métis, revenues generated by these occupations were crucial to their material well being. A decline in the supply of any one of them could easily spell increased and noticeable material hardship. The precariousness of their livelihood was further determined by the prices for these goods (furs, berries, roots) that fluctuated wildly; frequently, events that adversely affected fishing often had an impact on the prices of these commodities. For example in 1914–15 Inspector Jackson wrote:

> The price of fur has been very low this season—muskrats about 10 cents each; and to show what a drag [*sic*] in the market furs are, one reliable Indian informed me that he took some muskrat skins into the H.B.C.'s store and they refused to buy at any price.[61]

The year 1914 coincided with a downward trend in fish prices and the income generated by berry picking or harvesting seneca root could not be increased sufficiently to compensate for loss of revenue in other sectors.[62] These were also times when the fishermen-farmers with large outfits would be cutting back on their labour needs, trying to weather the "down" years. The Fort Rouge "Métis," neither fully staples producers nor fully wage labourers, suffered the most when an economic slump affecting both spheres occurred. Even in good years they were never in a position to improve their material conditions sufficiently to change their ethnic status, that is, to become French Canadians.

"C'est pas beau être Métis,"[1]
1901–1914

A T SOME POINT BETWEEN 1850 AND 1914, "Métis" became a derogatory term. It described people holding marginal social and economic positions on the shores of lakes Manitoba and Winnipegosis. Prior to 1850, "Métis" described people of native and European heritage who, by and large, supplied food staples (pemmican, fish, salt) to the fur trade companies and who were, occasionally, a source of cheap labour, first for the North West Company and, after 1821, for the Hudson's Bay Company. Other social and economic groups of the northwestern interior emerging after 1821—petty traders and eventually farmers—appeared to have little or no objections to being labelled Métis. This is true even though, by 1870, their way of thinking and their way of seeing the world were quite different from the larger hunting-and-fishing segment.

Initial uneasiness with the concept of "Métiness" appears on the shores of the two lakes in the 1880s. By 1880, many of the old lakeshore families were trapped in lives of poverty and recurrent hunger, caused by lack of land, little or no access to capital and none of the knowledge necessary for a transition to a farming-and-fishing lifestyle. After 1880, families who had succeeded in achieving a relatively comfortable living began distancing themselves from their impoverished neighbours and relatives by emphasising their French-Canadian background and rejecting the label "Métis." As the Delaronde-Boyer example illustrates, some respondents flatly rejected the idea that they, their parents or their grandparents were Métis. They readily agreed that they had a "pretty mixed" background but stated categorically they were not "Métis." The Delaronde-Boyer comment that the old grandmother, Marie Anne Delaronde, did not allow her children to play with those she considered "Métis" strengthens the argument that, by 1910, the parameters of being Métis were coming to be defined culturally and economically rather than by ancestry. Being of mixed ancestry was not the same as being Métis!

This book explores to what degree an analysis, emphasising the importance of life experiences and choices, material conditions and the emergence of different social classes in the second half of the 19th century, contributes to a better understanding of "Métis" history on the shores of Lakes Manitoba and Winnipegosis. Several quite serious caveats apply to the data. There is a dearth in archival materials available for the Saint-Laurent region. For example, there are no pre-World War II municipal tax assessment rolls extant. Finally, there are all of the problems inherent upon relying on oral history as a source of data. Despite these caveats, some conclusions can be drawn with reasonable confidence.

The penetration of new economic, social and ideological influences in the Saint-Laurent area after 1870 did have a direct and in some cases terrible effect on a portion of the population listed as "Métis" in the first general census of the region. But what is important to note is that it was not a blanket effect; not all of the old families were adversely affected. As discussed in the previous chapters, many of the old Red River families (especially those arriving in Saint-Laurent after 1880) and some of the "northern" Métis families prospered in the Canadian phase of this region's history. The simple, crucial and contradictory facts of both persistence and assimilation escape the notice of many researchers dealing with "Métis" history. They fail to notice the changes in the use of the term between 1870 and 1914. It is argued here that the change in nuances of meaning underlying the term "Métis" can be traced to changes in the economy of the region, and the varied impact of these changes upon different groups within the early population. In other words, hunters were affected differently than merchants. Also of importance was the importation of a racist ideology having its roots in the development of both British and French society.[2] Racist precepts and ideas provided a simple "visual" explanatory framework for phenomena and conditions actually produced or rooted in complex changes in economic forces.

In 1850, the lakeshore dwellers could already be grouped in three socio-economic strata. First, there was the much-discussed Cree- and French(*Mitchif*)-speaking trading families who made a living buying pelts, pemmican and salt from the other two groups for resale to the large fur companies. Second, there was the large, nebulous and elusive group labelled as Freemen Métis, who lived a life of hunting, fishing and small-scale trading and trapping. The Freemen were a group that migrated along the Duck Bay, Saint-Laurent, *au large* (White Mud River effluent) circuit. Many had ties to Father Belcourt's Saulteaux village. Their cultural, ideological, and political ties to the Red River Métis population (even its bison-hunting segment) appear to have been weak. The Freemen Métis spoke Cree and Saulteaux with equal ease but missionaries often note their poor knowledge of French. Finally, the longest residing settlers in the area were the Saulteaux Indians, who dwelt largely at the northern end of Lake Manitoba and on the shores of Lake Winnipegosis, gaining their livelihood through hunting and trapping. Though linked to the Metis population through marital and economic ties, they remained by and large a distinct community at the end of the period under study.

It is difficult to know how the trading families considered the Freemen prior to the 1870s. The traders certainly appear to have had little or no objection to being labelled "Métis" alongside Freemen. However, their insistence upon placing distinctions between themselves and the Indian segment of the population could be quite virulent. Though their trading activities led them to marital alliances (though rarely formal or long term) with the Saulteaux, they were adamant in maintaining a distinction to the point of refusing to let their Saulteaux "in-laws" raise their children. Also, in the early 1870s, trading Métis appear to have forced families they considered to be "Indian" out of the Saint-Laurent-Oak Point area. Clearly, the traders considered the "Indian" segment of the population to be socially apart and economically beneath them. The Indians were a group with whom one had business and affective ties but with which one did not permanently cohabit or merge. This distancing was not due to the mere fact that the Indians were Saulteaux as opposed to Cree speakers (i.e., different "ethnic" groups), since people of French-Canadian, Scottish, and Irish descent had little or no difficulty in merging with the trading elite.

How the Freemen reacted to the Métis-Saulteaux distinction is unclear. Since they spent more time with the Saulteaux in the Duck Bay area than with the traders at Fond du Lac, one could conclude that distinctions were not as rigidly maintained.

Certainly the Saint-Laurent marriage registers for the northern missions note the marriages of several Métis men and women with recently baptised people having Saulteaux names. Unlike the majority of the trading element, the Freemen appear to have been willing to have their marriages to "Indians" regularised, perhaps because they viewed these to be of a long-term nature. Certainly, the Oblates never mention one of these Freemen having simultaneously a "real" Métis wife and "Indian" concubine.

In the three decades following the annexation of Manitoba to Canada, the social structure of the Lake Manitoba and Lake Winnipegosis population changed radically. Unlike the situation in the older and more southerly parishes, a key element of change was not so much the large-scale arrival of out-of-province migrants but rather a gradual change in the area's economy, coupled with the arrival of Métis families from the more southerly Red River parishes. The initial wave came in 1868–69 during a famine year. These were families who, though destitute, had some knowledge of agrarian pursuits and an awareness of the potential value of landed property. They, along with some members of the old trading families, laid claim to individual river lots in 1872 and again in 1874. The Freemen Métis did not, for reasons which are difficult to determine. Lack of interest in, or comprehension of, private property may be part of the reason, but a less subjective explanation is their absence in the spring of 1872 when the Wagner survey was made. Most would still have been in their wintering site of Duck Bay. A second explanation would be their inability to fulfil the residency requirements: a problem also plaguing several traders. Many Métis Freemen and traders had never erected permanent dwellings at Fond du Lac even though they considered the area their home base. The Freemen lived in Saint-Laurent between May and October when wooden structures were superfluous.

Why so few individuals from the trading families filed a written claim to land is more problematic.[3] They were certainly aware, from their frequent visits to the Red River Settlement and the preaching of the Oblates, that changes were pending after 1870. As with the Freemen, inability to meet the list of settlement duties ("improvements") and simple *hivernage* absences were part of the problem. It is crucial to remember that for the trading families well into the 1880s there was a viable, even lucrative, alternative to farming. It is fairly obvious from Wagner's residency maps that these families saw a river lot as a *pied-à-terre*, a place to build a house, to have a small store or to run a saloon, but not as a place to farm or ranch on any scale. They made a comfortable living trading and freighting. It is probable that they simply misjudged the rapidity with which the farming-fishing economy would displace the fur trade on the south shores of Lake Manitoba and the scale at which the large fur and fish companies would monopolise commerce and trading along the full length of both lakes. It was not ignorance or unwillingness to change that eventually led many of the children of the original trading families to a life of poverty after 1880, but rather a collective error in judgement.

The Métis families who chose a life of farming coupled with fishing prior to the 1880s may have gained the approval of the clergy, but they condemned themselves

François (Frank) Chartrand and family, accompanied by an unidentified Oblate priest, at Duck Bay, early 20th century. The house in the background is typical of the type used by "winterers."

to several years of struggle and hardship. The clergy's letters are filled with concerned remarks about early frosts, locusts, lack of markets and difficulties in transporting cheese and butter over oxcart trails. Cash income was derived largely from ice fishing, just as for the Freemen. The key difference between the two groups was that the farmers were able to retain a measure of independence vis-à-vis the merchants because they did not depend on them for basic foodstuffs. As the priests noted, all the lakeshore dwellers had become dependent upon flour, pork, lard, butter, and canned goods. These Freemen had to buy whether the fishing was remunerative or not. The farming element could produce at least part of their own foodstuffs and sell off their farming surpluses to obtain other "needed" goods such as tea or sugar. The Freemen, on the other hand, were completely dependent upon the merchants and this, the priests noted disapprovingly, led to a perpetual cycle of debt and the frequent threat of famine.

The *apparent* rejection by the Freemen Métis of the *habitant* lifestyle coupled to their social habits of public drinking and partying, combined with their disregard for church authorities, led to their social marginalisation—first by the church authorities and then by the "respectable" fishing and farming families. Oblates increasingly refer to the two groups as "good" and "bad" Métis families, with the traders holding an ambiguous in-between position.[4]

Among the families that were becoming "white" in the 1880s was a large contingent of old Manitoba families originating mainly from the southern parishes. It is well documented that a significant number of Métis who attempted to stay, claim their lands, and farm after 1870, left their farms in the 1880s.[5] They appear to have become disheartened by the actions of speculators, the slowness of the government in dealing with their claims and, perhaps, the attitudes of newcomers. Not all headed west; several Red River families from the older parishes went to Saint-Laurent. They arrived there with some small measure of capital. The majority bought land outright or they successfully homesteaded. Their arrival immediately precedes the improvement in road transportation, the expansion of the railway in the area, and the opening of local outlets (cheese and butter factories) for dairy products. Although not necessarily causally related to the appearance of the new immigrants, the development of the region's infrastructure assured them a measure of material success in their new home.

It was usually the Red River families who, from 1880 to 1914, increased the social, economic and even physical distance (with the formation of Fort Rouge) between themselves and their hunting-and-gathering brethren. These Red River families, along with the clergy, out-of-province migrants, and some of the older local well-to-do families, began to redefine what "Métis" meant. Though several aged respondents from Saint-Laurent readily admitted to having Indian ancestors, they vehemently denied being "Métis." They honestly believe themselves to be French Canadians. To be "Métis" was to be poor, to live in a run-down shack in Fort Rouge, and to cling to pre-1870 customs of dress, language, social and economic values. To be "Métis" was to be disrespectful of the clergy, indifferent to Catholic dogma, and unaware of the value of education. But, most important, to be "Métis" in Saint-Laurent in 1914 meant not to own land or livestock and not to be at least a part-time farmer.

In all fairness, differences between the Fort Rouge and farming "Métis" may have had roots in pre-1870 attitudes. It is possible the trading families of Fond du Lac had felt some difference between themselves and their lakeshore hunting-and-gathering counterparts prior to 1870. Certainly the more established Red River and Saint-François Xavier families coming up in 1868 and later would have perceived differences between themselves and the Freemen Métis. The Red River families did not have any close ties to the Lake Winnipegosis and Lake Manitoba Saulteaux, were more knowledgeable of farming, and were less able to seasonally move to Duck Bay or elsewhere. As they themselves noted, they were not "as Indian" as Freemen Métis. In fact, the latecomers were so "un-Indian" there are indications that the Freemen did not even consider them to be "Métis." Yet, when one looks at the genealogies of all of the pre-1890 Saint-Laurent families, they are nearly identical—"French-Canadian" father or grandfather and "Indian" mother or grandmother. The only genealogical difference was a slightly greater propensity for Freemen Métis to have official "Indian" wives in the 1870s and 1880s. The key variable which determined who became French Canadian and who remained "Métis" was the ability, in the decade 1870 to 1880, to acquire and exploit land; in short, the new definition of Métis implied a failed integration into the provincial dairy economy.

Who remained "Métis" after 1870 in the Lake Winnipegosis and Lake Manitoba region? By and large, the initial core was composed of the Freemen who lived a life of fishing and gathering along the shores of Lake Manitoba and Lake Winnipegosis, with occasional forays into the White Mud River district for bison or moose hunting. Independent, apparently with little or no direct ties to the old Red River parishes (outside the Saulteaux village) or the Hudson's Bay Company (either for commercial or wage labour), they identified closely with the local Saulteaux population. Certainly, they married into this tribe (unlike most of the traders, these were long-term marital arrangements) and, as frequently noted by the clergy, they spoke Saulteaux with much greater ease than French, if they knew the latter at all.

The majority of the Freemen were never in a position to lay claim to river lots. They were often absent at the times of the surveys and censuses. Most never made European improvements (house, barn, fence) to parcels of lands they considered their own. Clerical correspondence notes the arrival of other such families who lived day-to-day throughout the 1870s, as bison returns dwindled to nothing and small-scale fishing became the only viable alternative for those without capital. Geographically and socially segregated, these Métis families continued to produce a variety of goods specifically for exchange: primarily frozen fish but also seneca root, pelts, berries and other "forest" and "wild" products. From the merchants, the hunting-and-gathering Métis received basic foodstuffs, clothes, and the tools necessary to pursue their trade. Such exchanges were never favourable enough for these Métis to get out of debt and to begin to accumulate the capital, land, livestock and equipment necessary for farming and large-scale ice fishing.

These Métis hunting, gathering, and fishing families worked year round, but their economic pursuits did not enable them to participate in the provincial dairy-farm economy except as poorly paid seasonal labourers. Such economic activities also assured these Métis a position of marginality in the international fishing economy. In some cases economic and social marginality translated into a retreat northward and, sometimes, a total merging with the Indian population by the acquisition of treaty status.

Trapped in social, economic, and geographical isolation, the Fort Rouge "Métis" maintained their pre-1870 customs, habits, worldview and traditions. Farming families that aspired to becoming French Canadian consciously suppressed these traits and hid them from their children. Most farming respondents noted that even though their parents and grandparents had known an "Indian" language, they were careful not to speak it to their children and grandchildren. The Fort Rouge "Métis" certainly had no such compulsions as late as the 1920s. In the years following the turn of the century, poverty in Fort Rouge *maintained* social, cultural and linguistic traits that differed more and more from the norm found in the farming element of Lake Manitoba and Lake Winnipegosis. These traits, and their origins in a dual heritage and fur-trade economy, began to be seen as the explanation for, as opposed to the result of, a marginal existence. This belief, which was held by the less marginal Saint-Laurent inhabitants, conveniently ignored the fact that surprising numbers of "French-Canadian" and "Breton" farming families in the Saint-Laurent area had ancestors who, prior to 1870, considered themselves "Métis." "Métis" had ceased to designate a nation and had become a class.

The dynamics of expanding capitalism, coupled to a growing European racist ideology, produced a marginalised class on the shores of Lake Manitoba and Lake Winnipegosis. Many former colonies have such reserve labour forces. These people lived partly off the land and partly from low-wage seasonal employment, especially prior to World War I. Most individuals did not live so precariously, hand to mouth, by choice. In Manitoba, when industrial jobs became available there was a distinct tendency to abandon seasonal work in favour of employment that produced more predictable returns.[6] In Saint-Laurent, as in most of the Interlake region, this class became viewed as racially or ethnically distinct. This was because of a series of specific social, economic and historical circumstances that affected livelihoods and reinforced an emerging racist ideology. Slight physical variations were negatively evaluated and the evaluation (for Manitoba Métis in 20% of the cases) reinforced the very real impact of chronic material hardship. It became part of society's common perception that "most poor people in the area were Native, and that most Natives were poor." To this day, the authorities, the public, and even the people affected, think in terms of "Indian and Métis" problems, or of injustices done to "Natives." They posit solutions with ethnic boundaries in mind, not realising that they are buying into a racist perspective. Such a way of seeing things displaces critical analysis away from very real economic and social issues. The problem is not one of ancestorship. The precise difficulty for a group of lakeshore residents, especially between 1870 and 1914, was that the occupations allowing them to survive and feed their families also guaranteed it would be next to impossible for them to improve their material conditions and those of their children. Hunting, fishing and seasonal work trapped them into a life of poverty.

Endnotes

Introduction

1. Dennis F.K. Madill, "Riel, Red River and Beyond: New Developments in Metis History," in Colin G. Calloway (ed.), *New Directions in American History* (Norman, OK: University of Oklahoma Press, 1987), 19–78; Fritz Pannekoek, "Metis Studies: The Development of a Field and New Directions," in Theodore Binnema, Gerhard J. Ens and R.C. Macleod (eds.), *From Rupert's Land to Canada* (Edmonton: University of Alberta Press, 2001) 111–28. For an example of the study of a specific "non-Red River Métis" community see Gavin Kerr et Nicole St-Onge, "Une communauté migratoire frontalière: Les voyageurs de Penetanguishene, 1796–1828," *Cahiers franco-canadiens de l'Ouest* 12 (2000): 29–46.

2. Jennifer Brown, "People of Myth, People of History: A Look at Recent Writing on the Metis," *Acadiensis* 17 (1987): 150–62.

3. Ibid, 150.

4. J.R. Miller, "From Riel to the Metis," *Canadian Historical Review* 69 (1988): 17.

5. Ibid.

6. Pannekoek, "Metis Studies," 111.

7. In 1868, a famine year, colonial and ecclesiastical authorities conducted detailed surveys of the inhabitants and their economic assets.

8. 1881, being a census year, is used as a watershed year to compare and contrast the community as portrayed by the 1871 census.

9. Jean H. Lagassé, *The People of Indian Ancestry in Manitoba: A Social and Economic History*, Vol. 1 (Winnipeg: Dept. of Agriculture and Immigration, 1959), 77.

Chapter 1

1. Hudson Bay Company Archives (hereafter HBCA), Provincial Archives of Manitoba (hereafter PAM), B.235/a/8 folio 14, page 24. The Métis were doing a booming trade buying furs in the Lake Manitoba region and reselling them at 100% profit to the Company.

2. A. Morice, *History of the Catholic Church in Canada*, 2 vols. (Toronto: The Mission Book Company, 1919), 118.

3. *Nor'Wester*, April 28, 1860.

4. Marcel Giraud, *Le Métis Canadien*, with a foreword by J.E. Foster (Paris: Institut d'ethnologie, 1945; Saint-Boniface, MB: 1984), 1012–28.

5. This kin-based social and economic network leading to varying degrees of distinctiveness has been well documented in various individual regional and temporal studies. Peterson wrote on the role of the mixed-blood families in the Great Lakes. Tanis C. Thorne uses the concept of extended mixed families as "guilds" in her analysis of the roles of the Missouri Métis (*The Many Hands of My Relations*, 137). Also Heather Divine in "Les Desjarlais" and John E. Foster in "Wintering, the Outside Adult Male and the Ethnogenesis of the Western Plains Métis" discuss the creation of a Freemen role and its impact on Métis identity.

6. James M. Richtik, "A Historical Geography of the Interlake Area of Manitoba from 1871 to 1921" (MA thesis, University of Manitoba, 1964), 19.

7. "Reminiscences of Father Bousquet" in Pauline Mercier, *Renseignements sur Saint-Laurent, Manitoba* (Elie, MB: Division Scolaire de la Prairie du Cheval Blanc, 1974), 54. Apparently, as parish priest in the 1930s, Bousquet interviewed village elders.

8. "Daily, families who have no other resources for obtaining their subsistence during winter, leave the settlement for Lake Manitoba, or the Grand Forks." PAM, HBCA, B235/a/9, Fort Garry Journal, page 13, October 10, 1827.

   "Pendant ces années de détresse (1818–1825) toute la population vécut de la pêche ou de la viande des buffles. Le froid de l'hiver nous donnait le moyen de la manger fraiche et en été séchée au soleil ou au feu. Le sel qu'on fait dans le pays en était le seul assaisonnement." National Archives of Canada, MG 17 A22 (F840), Association de la Propagation de la Foi (Paris), 1 February 1836, "Notice sur la Mission de Saint-Boniface de la Rivière Rouge."

9. Giraud, *Le Métis Canadien*, 648.

10. Gerhard J. Ens, *Homeland to Hinterland: The Changing Worlds of the Red River Métis in the Nineteenth Century* (Toronto: University of Toronto Press, 1996), 49.

11. "J'ai trouvé une occasion hier par John Cyr de venir dire la messe aux pêcheurs de St-Boniface et de St-Norbert. J'avais une respectable assistance au Saint Sacrifice ce matin et rien que du français!" Archives de l'Archevêché de Saint-Boniface (hereafter AASB), T5909–T5912, Lestanc à Taché, Vieille Pêche, November 18, 1868.

12. Giraud, *Le Métis Canadien*, 781.

13. Ens, *Homeland to Hinterland,* 73–92.

14. "Il y a un troisieme hivernement à la Riviere Blanche et c'est de là que j'ai l'honneur d'écrire a votre Grâce… Ici tous les chasseurs ne sont pas encore arrivés de la prairie; ils vont arriver demain ou après demain et l'on pense que le camp comptera quarante maisons." AASB, T11168-T11171, Lestanc à Taché, Rivière Blanche, November 13, 1872.

15. For example, according to his grandson, Etienne Delaronde worked for years for the HBC hauling freight, mail and provisions on (his own?) barges. The route went from Winnipeg, Portage La Prairie, Delta, up to Lake Winnipegosis. Etienne Delaronde married Helen Monkman whom he had met while working on Lake Winnipeg. They first lived near Rabbit Point, west of Vogar, on the shores of Lake Manitoba. At a later date Etienne quit the HBC freighting business and started a ranch at "Maryhill" west of Lundar (also near the lake). He eventually relocated his family, permanently, at Coteau de Roche, a small settlement ("suburb") near Saint-Laurent and continued to ranch. In the 1870 census Etienne Delaronde, age 9, had been listed as residing with his family in Saint-Laurent. His parents were Etienne Laronde, a trader, and Julienne Carrière—son and granddaughter of French-Canadian fur trade employees. This pattern of movement and relocation along the shores of Lake Manitoba (and Winnipegosis) seems common for a large segment of the Saint-Laurent population during the period examined. Michif Language Committee (hereafter MLC), tape 9, side 1, September 8, 1987.

16. Giraud, *Le Métis Canadien,* 832.

17. SHSB, P3319-P3335, Belcourt to Cazeau, July 21, 1840.

18. AASB, T5270–T5285, Simonet to Taché, February 8, 1868 (mentions Métis from Saint-Laurent "hivernant à la Saline").

19. Henry Youle Hind, *Narrative of the Canadian Red River Exploring Expedition of 1857 and of the Assiniboine and Sakatchewan Expedition of 1858*, vol. 2 (London: Longman, Green, Longman and Roberts, 1860), 41.

20. SHSB, P3319-P3335, Belcourt to Cazeau, July 21, 1840

21. In the 1870 census he is listed as a half-breed but Morice labels him a *Canadien* (Quebecer) in his works. A.G. Morice, *Dictionnaire des Canadiens et Métis Français de l'Ouest* (Saint-Boniface, 1908).

22. Oblats de Marie Immaculée (OMI), Archives Deschatelet (AD), L381 M27C 1858–1895, Historical Notes, Parish of Saint-Laurent.

23. OMI, AD, L381 M27C 1858-1895, Historical Notes, Parish of Saint-Laurent.

24. Herman G. Sprenger, "An Analysis of Selected Aspects of Métis Society, 1810–1870" (MA thesis, University of Manitoba, 1972).

25. Most of the genealogical data is gleaned from: 1) D.N. Sprague and R.P. Frye, *The Genealogy of the First Métis Nation* or the six volume publication by Gail Morin, *Métis Families A Genealogical Compendium* (Pawtucket: Quintin Publications, 2001); 2) the Executive Relief Committee statistical summary (parish of Saint-Laurent); 3) the 1870 and 1891 censuses; 4) the river lot files; 5) the survey made of the parish of Saint-Laurent by the local priest (visite de paroisse) in 1910; 6) Oblate correspondence generally; and 7) oral history notes. Original sources take precedence.

26. Pierre "Bostonois" Pangman was the son of a North West Company bourgeois of German descent (Peter) from Elisebeth Town, NJ. Peter Pangman (1794–1819) would retire in the Montreal area purchasing the seigneury of Lachenaie. He initially was active in the Mississippi fur trade but eventually expanded his activities as far north as York Factory. Both Pierre "Bostonois" and son were active supporters of the NWC during its rivalry with the HBC. Pierre "Bostonois" Pangman was a highly respected man among the bison-hunting population.

27. HBCA, North West Company Ledger 1811–1821 (hereafter NWCL) F4/32, Pierre Pangman entry.

28. Gail Morin, *Censuses of the Red River Settlement* (Pawtucket: Quintin Publications, 1998).

29. Marguerite Pangman was married to Michel Chartrand and her sister, Marie, was married to his brother, Pierre.

30. The move to Duck Bay occurred in the winter of 1858–59. That winter, ecclesiastical records note, Elizabeth, the daughter of Pierre Pangman, was spending quite a bit of time with the newly arrived priests at Fond du Lac. This came to an abrupt end when her father came to take her back to Duck Bay where he had built a residence. The chronicler notes that she was able to return several times to visit the priests and made a point of having her marriage to Norbert Chaboyer performed in Saint-Laurent in October 1867.

31. It is sometimes difficult to ascertain, when sources speak of people being Cree, Saulteaux or French speakers, whether they are referring to the original languages or the Cree-French, Saulteaux-French, and French-mitchif fur-trade variants. For information derived from the oral sources a judgment call had to be made by this author. However, the Oblates writing between 1850 and 1914 would have been familiar enough with these linguistic nuances to label the spoken word accurately. Their descriptions and labelling of the languages they heard are accepted as accurate.

32. There is some discrepancy between the 1870 census, the Sprague-Frye genealogical reconstruction, and a small published history of the parish on the first name of this ancestor. Information from the 1870 census ("name of father"), was used in this work. All sources agree that his wife was Native (not Métis).

33. AASB P0756-0757. Darveau, Voyages d'automne à St-Norbert, 1843; quoted in Martha McCarthy, *To Evangelize the Nations: Roman Catholic Missions in Manitoba, 1818–1870* (Winnipeg, Historical Resources Branch Report, 1987), 110, 115.

34. A settlement founded by Father Belcourt on the banks of the Assiniboine for the local

Indian population. Housing several Métis families, it would eventually become Baie St-Paul.

35. Giraud, *Le Métis Canadien*, 846.

36. PAM, MG2 B6 1868 Statistical Summary, Executive Relief Committee, District of Assiniboia (parish of Saint-Laurent).

37. Though these "lakeshore" or "northern" Métis did some bison hunting in the Riding Mountain area (affluent of the White Mud River) there is no evidence to indicate their involvement in the large-scale bison hunting expedition originating from Saint-Norbert or Saint-François Xavier after their move to Saint-Laurent. Their *point de mire* from an economic point was the north shore of Lake Manitoba and Lake Winnipegosis (Duck Bay).

38. OMI, AD, L381 M27C 1858–1895, Historical notes, Parish of Saint-Laurent, pp. 1–2.

39. This would be a source of anxiety to the clergy in the years to come, as is seen in AASB, T14639, Camper à Taché, Saint-Laurent, July 26, 1874:

Il me peine extrêmement d'être obligé de dire à votre grâce qu'il ma été impossible de faire faire la première communion aux enfants… Je ne saurais les admettre a une si sainte action avec de pareilles dispositions. Je ne puis pas me damner par vaine complaisance pour eux autres. Parmi les grandes personnes il n'y a guère plus de zèle pour s'approcher des sacrements.

It distresses me greatly to have to tell your eminence that it was impossible for me to give the first communion to the children… I cannot admit them to such a sacred rite with their dispositions. I cannot damn my soul just to please them. Amongst the adults, I see no greater zeal to partake in the holy sacraments.

40. Michel Chartrand gave the priest $50 towards the building of the chapel as a sign of repentance after the incident mentioned above. The fact that he was in a position to give such an amount indicates that the Chartrand family was probably involved in trading activities.

41. AASB, T1659–T1662, Simonet à Taché, Pointe de Chêne, September 26, 1862. It is possible that the Baptiste married to Mary Messiapit, according to the 1870 census, is Paul Chartrand Jr.'s son. The Baptiste Chartrand who was involved with both Métis and Indian women (Paul Chartrand's brother) had already moved permanently to the Duck Bay area by the year of the census. Genealogical complexities aside, the data indicates the continued close ties kept by these lakeshore Métis with the fur trapping population well into the second half of the nineteenth century—a trend not as evident in the more established Métis population living on the banks of the Red River.

42. AASB, T1566-T1567, Simonet à Taché, Lac Manitoba, August 4, 1862.

43. AASB, T0864-T0867, Simonet à Taché, Pointe de Chêne, September 26, 1861:

A l'aide du peu de Cri que j'ai appris cet été à St-Boniface, j'ai pu entendre les confessions de près de cinquante personnes dont deux ou trois seulement parlaient le français, un en anglais. J'ai fait tous les jours le cathéchisme et l'école en Cri.

With the help of the little Cree I learned this summer in Saint-Boniface I was able to hear the confessions of close to fifty people of which only two or three spoke French and one spoke English. Every day I teach catechism and school in Cree.

44. Not all the Métis closely allied to the Saulteaux population moved north. Antoine Chartrand married to "Frances" of Duck River was, among others, still listed as living in Oak Point in 1870.

45. Saint-François Xavier is the parish name given to the old settlement of Grantown.

46. Data collected from PAM, Executive Relief Report, MG2 B6 1868, Saint-Laurent Parish.

47. In a normal year the Lavallées would have planted 12 bushels of potatoes producing on average a yield of 384 bushels, since one bushel planted produces 32 bushels harvested (personal communication, Milton museum of agriculture).

48. There is no direct information stating that the Lavallées were traders. In fact oral tradition describes them as active fishermen and (post-1900) good dairy farmers. Unfortunately, this data goes back only to the post-1880 period when trading opportunities had already begun to diminish seriously (and the market for fish to expand).

49. Louise Chartrand was a sister to the previously mentioned Michel and Baptiste.

50. By 1870 there was a Ducharme family residing in Saint-Laurent but the link-up to Josèphte is not clear. This was the family of Jean-Baptiste Ducharme and Catherine Allary.

51. Nicolas Ducharme's brother Antoine Ducharme is listed as residing in the Saulteaux village in 1843 and owning a house, a stable, 2 mares, an ox, 2 carts, a canoe and cultivating 2 acres. According to available genealogies Antoine would have children with three women: the first two Métis (Josette Villebrun and Josette Richard), and the last an Indian women called Josette Mackegone. François Richard, the father of his second wife Josette Richard, is also listed as a resident of the Saulteaux village in 1843.

52. He was born c. 1795 and died in Saint-Laurent in 1868.

53. Catherine Pangman was the daughter of Pierre "Bostonais" Pangman and Marguerite Sauteuse. They married January 14, 1851 in St. François-Xavier. Not enough data existed to construct an accurate family chart for the Sayer clan.

54. Mercier, *Renseignements sur Saint-Laurent, Manitoba,* 17.

55. Giraud, *Le Métis Canadien,* 920.

56. They were not present during the census of 1871 but they would be listed as "from the parish of Saint-Laurent on the 1878 marriage certificate of their son William to Rose Carrière.

57. HBCA, PAM, B.235/a/8 folio 14, January 1827.

58. "Nos traiteurs partent et sont remplacés par les pêcheurs qui viennent tous les jours." AASB, T5832–T5834, Simonet à Taché, Lac Manitoba, 20 September 1868.

59. Their Cree may have been some form of Cree-mitchif simply not recognised as such by the missionaries used to Red River Mitchif. The Métisses, especially, did not quickly pick up French: "Bien des femmes surtout ne parlent que le sauvage." AASB, P3862–P3866, Provencher à Proulx, June 5, 1842.

60. Jerome Lavallée, a retired farmer-fisherman-trapper of Saint-Laurent, stated in an interview with the author in 1984 that his grandfather, Michel Lavallée, spoke only Cree and Saulteaux ("but he understood French"). Jérome's father, Joseph (Michel) Lavallée, spoke Cree, Saulteaux and French "fluently." Jérome speaks Cree, Saulteaux, French and English. He notes that his wife, Florence Lafrenière, is (Métis) Cree and she refuses to speak Saulteaux (which Jérome defines as "his" language) because she pronounces the words "all crooked" and the interviewee laughs at her! Michel Lavallée's (the grandfather) parents were the above-mentioned Jean Baptiste Lavallée and Louise Ducharme.

Also, Marie Louise (Lavallée) Walstrom, born in Saint-Laurent in 1905, commented in a 1984 interview with the author that her parents, Baptiste Lavallée of Saint-Laurent and Catherine Chartrand of Clarkleigh, spoke "Saulteaux and French all mixed up." Her paternal grandparents were André Lavallée and "Lissa" (Eliza) Chaboyer, and maternal grandparents were Michel Chartrand and Marguerite Pangman. This statement would seem to conflict with comments found in the missionary letters on the "Cree" spoken by the "Métis." Perhaps what she describes as "French" is the michif Cree alluded to by the Oblates. Or else, by the turn of the century, several "Métis" families were speaking Saulteaux as opposed to their old Cree dialect.

61. That distinct "Métis" and "Native" groups reproduced themselves does not mean that individuals were not "passing" and merging with the other group. It is interesting to note that, by the 1870 census, only four Métis living in Saint-Laurent had "official" wives that were listed as being Indian. Either the Native wives (official or unofficial) were staying up north and the official Métis household resided at the mission or the former "Indians" were declaring themselves to be "Métis." The first seems more likely since for the next 50 years the Oblates would speak with dismay of Métis going north and continuing to cause "scandal" (in their eyes only it would seem).

62. Nicole St-Onge, "Memories of Métis Women of Saint-Eustache," Oral History Forum, 19–20 (1999–2000): 91–112.

63. Neither the Interlake Cree-Métis nor the Saulteaux were highly regarded by the priest. There are many negative references to the Lake Manitoba Saulteaux found in missionary correspondence: "Vraiment ces sauteux sont une race maudite de Dieu, il me faut la foi pour dire qu'ils sont faits a l'image de Dieu et capables de prendre place dans le ciel." AASB, GLP327, Bermond à Faraud, Fond du lac, May 10, 1850. Letters lamenting the lakeshore Métis' lack of religious concern abound in the Religious Archives. See for example: AASB, T5832–T5834, Simonet à Taché, Lac Manitoba, September 20, 1868.

64. AASB, T5270–T5285, Simonet à Taché, Saint-Laurent, February 8, 1868. Duck Bay was the earliest Roman Catholic effort at establishing an at least nominally permanent mission in the Lake Winnipegosis region. In 1838, the priest Father Belcourt was attempting to settle the neighbouring Saulteaux in this area (with mixed results). Duck Bay had always been a traditional fall gathering place and the nearby salt springs were a further asset. With the years, more and more Métis families were wintering here (as the buffalo disappeared from "la montagne" [the upper White Mud river area]). In the late summer of 1858 Hind visited the area and found 40 to 50 "halfbreed" Indians living there. This would seem to indicate that the original Saulteaux and Cree evangelised by Darveau and Belcourt were absorbed or replaced by Métis. These Métis were living a life similar to that of the fur trapping segment of the population, since Hind said these people grew only a few potatoes because their fish and game provided such abundant food. Métis traders and salt makers following a well-established circuit would also have had no time or need for gardening. In the winter of 1868, according to Father Simonet, there were 22 "Catholic" families wintering in the Duck Bay-"Les Salines" area not counting "les traiteurs ou autres hivernants qui viennent de la Rivière Rouge ou de la Prairie du Cheval Blanc." AASB, T5270–T5285, Simonet à Taché, Saint-Laurent, February 8, 1868. For more details consult: Martha McCarthy, *Pre-1870 Roman Catholic Missions in Manitoba* (Winnipeg: Historical Resources Branch Report, 1987).

65. AASB, T5942–T5945, Simonet à Taché, Saint-Laurent, October 29, 1868.

66. In the census of 1840, the last in which he appears, James Monkman (68) is listed as owning a horse, 4 stables, 2 barns, 4 mares, 4 oxen, 7 cows, 3 calves, 8 pigs, 60 sheep, 3 ploughs, 3 harrows, 6 carts, 2 canoes, a boat, and 30 acres cultivated.

67. Their father, who continued his father's salt-making plant at Salt Springs on Lake Winnipegosis, helped Dr. J.C. Schultz escape to Ontario in 1870 and tried to "agitate"

certain elements against the Métis. In a letter discussing the amnesty question written on February 20, 1875, Louis Riel Jr. noted:

En même temps que des Ontariens commettaient ces actes d'agression violente dans le Fort Garry où ils étaient nos prisonniers de guerre, les sauvages du pays se trouvaient dans une grande agitation. Qui est-ce qui les agitait? Entr'autres un nommé Monkman, comme Scott à la solde du colonel Dennis, et qui avait reçu de cet agent du gouvernement canadien la mission de soulever les sauvages contres les anciens colons dont les établissement étaient ainsi exposés à des massacres barbares.

At the same time that the Ontarians committed these violent acts of aggression while they were our war prisoners in Fort Garry, the Indians of the country were in a state of great agitation. And who was agitating them? Amongst others, one named Monkman, who is like Scott in the employ of the major Dennis, and who had received from this agent of the Canadian government the mission to provoke an Indian uprising against the old settlers whose communities were thus exposed to barbarous massacres.

68. AASB, T5942–T5945, Simonet à Taché, Saint-Laurent, October 29, 1868.

69. AASB, T1566–T1567, Simonet à Taché, Lac Manitoba, August 4, 1862.

70. Ens, *Homeland to Hinterland*, 172–74. There would also be more traditional Freemen families such as the Chaboyer who would be in Fond du lac intermittently from the 1840s onwards and permanently from 1860 onward. They are listed in the 1843 Red River census as residents of the Saulteaux village with animals but no acreage. The head of the family, Louis Chaboyer, was married to Louise Chartrand also of a Saulteaux village/Fond du Lac family.

71. Fur trappers who, by the 1860–1870s, probably had as "mixed" a background as many of the Saint-Laurent and Oak Point dwellers.

72. Though some members of these families in the 20th century were involved in muskrat hunting as far North as Le Pas this did not seem to necessitate close ties with the local "Indian" population.

73. PAM, MG2 B6 1868, Statistical Summary, Executive Relief Committee, District of Assiniboia (parish of Saint-Laurent).

74. AASB, T5832–T5834, Simonet à Taché, Saint-Laurent, September 20, 1868.

75. A settlement on the western slopes of Duck Mountain also composed of non-Red River Settlement (i.e. "Freeman") Métis who, according to oral history, came up from Pembina and the Dakotas, and, interestingly, Baie St-Paul.

76. OMI, AD, L1074 M27L, Paroisse de Sainte Claire.

77. It is possible the famine did not have an immediate detrimental effect on trading and freighting families such as the Delarondes and the Chartrands. Goods still had to be moved along the lake, the market for salt was constant, and some fur animals were being caught. It is only when the trappers experienced difficulty finding food for themselves and the traders had none to exchange that business suffered.

Chapter 2

1. Most of the affluent members of the community (Chartrand, Delaronde, Monkman, etc.) would·be wintering on Lake Winnipegosis busy with trading, salt making, trapping, and fishing. By the 1860s log houses would have been built there rather than at Saint-Laurent and Oak Point.

2. Donald Gunn, "Notes of an Egging Expedition to Shoal Lake, West of Lake Winnipeg,"

Annual Report of the Board of Regents of the Smithsonian Institution for the Year 1867 (Washington: Government printers, 1872).

3. Also one of the principle sources of criticism emanating from the missionaries.

4. Gunn, "Notes," 431.

5. Ibid. (emphasis added). This tradition of autumn fishing on the shores of Lake Manitoba, often by residents of Saint-François Xavier and the Saulteaux village began much earlier. See Ens, *Homeland to Hinterland*, 49.

6. Gunn, "Notes," 431.

7. AASB, T5942-T5945, Simonet à Taché, Saint-Laurent, October 29, 1868.

8. Many of these people may have decided to spend a complete year (as opposed to a winter) on Lake Winnipegosis with their kin waiting out the calamities that were befalling the more southerly area.

9. As mentioned before, it is quite possible that individuals were merging with one or the other group during those difficult years.

10. J.M. Richtik in his "Historical Geography" uses Gunn's comments to argue that the Lake Manitoba Métis had become "very sedentary" and also that they were living at a subsistence level. These are erroneous conclusions for a significant proportion of the Lake Manitoba Métis. Missionary letters mention, well into the 20th century, established seasonal patterns of migration (Saint-Laurent, Duck Bay, White Mud River, Poste Manitoba and, later on, trapping at Le Pas and fishing on Great Slave Lake). It is possible there was a slight trend towards leaving Métis wives and children back at La Mission, but in the 1860s, most families followed their men north even when northern wives existed. To describe this population as functioning on a subsistence level is also, by and large, inaccurate. It was certainly inaccurate for the four (founding) families (and the Delarondes and Monkmans) who owned barges, engaged in trading and production for exchange, and hired employees. Even the Métis/Indian trappers and fishermen were producing as much for exchange as for consumption and, in good years, fetched a good price for their wares in the HBC post or the Red River Settlement. People whose means of existence force them into regular displacements do not acquire many material possessions but the appearance of marginality especially in difficult years, should not be equated with a subsistence level existence.

11. Pierre Pangman was listed as indigent in 1868. This is surprising since he was one of the earliest established traders in the Saint-Laurent area and he had extensive kin ties in Duck Bay. Old age may have been a factor. Unfortunately, there is not much data on this family either from written sources or from oral history. There are members of the Pangman family living in the Camperville-Duck Bay area to this day.

12. AASB, T5942–T5945, Simonet à Taché, Saint-Laurent, October 29, 1968.

13. Ibid.

14. The summer of 1868 was not a good fishing or hunting season even on Lake Winnipegosis. In the month of June the religious chronicles note that people were reduced to eating dried jackfish "hard as shingles" at Salt Springs.

15. AASB, T5499-T5502, Camper à Taché, Saint-Laurent, April 23, 1968.

16. OMI, AD, L381 M27C 1858-1895, Historical notes, Parish of Saint-Laurent.

17. AASB, T7270, Camper à Taché, Saint-Laurent, April 5, 1869.

18. One of these northern non-trading families was the "Guiboche" who wintered in 1869 with the "Parisien" at La Saline. One of their descendants in a taped interview noted that she had been told the Guiboche came from the northern end of the lake.

19. "Les hivernants du coté de la Baie des Canards commencent à arriver." AASB, T7477, Camper à Taché, Lac Manitoba, May 23, 1870.

20. "La pêche manque encore ce printemps comme à l'automne dernier." AASB, T7477, Camper à Taché, Lake Manitoba, May 23, 1870.

21. OMI, AD, L381 M27c 1858-1895 Historical Notes, Parish of Saint-Laurent.

22. AASB, T8170-T8173, Camper à Taché, Saint-Laurent, November 24, 1870.

23. "Viendra alors le temps des semences, Monseigneur, compter sur nos gens ce serait nous [condamner] à jeûner l'année qui vient." AASB, T8602–T8604, Camper à Taché, Saint-Laurent, March 28, 1871.

24. AASB, T8663, Proulx à Taché, Bout du Lac, April 15, 1871 (emphasis added).

25. AASB, T9332-35, Proulx à Taché, Bout du lac, September 12, 1871.

26. AASB, T9973-76, Camper à Taché, Saint-Laurent, February 15, 1872.

27. PAM, RG 17 C1 #258, Saint-Laurent, May 7 to May 13, 1872.

28. *Le Métis*, Vol. 1, no 2, 8 June 1871, "Saint-Laurent, Chronique de paroisse."

29. PAM, RG 17 C1 #257, Saint-Laurent, April 29 to May 6 1872.

30. PAM, RG 17 C1 #257, Oak Point, April 29 to May 13 1872.

31. *Le Métis*, June 8, 1871, page 2.

32. Gunn, "Notes," 427.

33. AASB, T10993–T1110, Camper à Taché, Saint-Laurent, October 1, 1872. Or again:

    Faites donc venir des catholiques des autres pays, me disait-il [Wagner] il y a quelque temps et laissez ces métis gagner le large et s'en aller dans le nord.

    "Bring Catholics from other countries," he [Wagner] was telling me a few days ago "and let these Métis go forth and head up North." AASB, T11517, Camper à Taché, Saint-Laurent, January 12, 1873.

34. Many possible reasons exist to explain the Saint-Laurent and Oak Point Métis traders and hivernants' usually late arrival (aside from break-up!). For example, they may have been waiting for an opportunity to trade with the Porcupine Hills "Indians":

    Les sauvages de la Montagne [Porcupine Hills] viennent faire le sucre tous les printemps près de la rivière Cygne puis ils vont au fort de Mr McBeath jusqu'au départ des barges [of the lake Manitoba Métis].

    *The Indians of the mountain [Porcupine Hills] come to make sugar near Swan River. Then they go to Mr. McBeath's fort and stay till the departure of the barges [of the Lake Manitoba Métis]. AASB, T6462, Camper à Taché, Saint-Laurent, April 7, 1869.

35. I assume he is counting heads of family. Unfortunately no mention is made of women and children.

36. PAM, RG17 C1 #258, Saint-Laurent, April 29 to May 6, 1872.

37. PAM, MG2 B3 M158, District of Assiniboia, Lake Manitoba.

38. These are male heads of family. Widows and their dependent seem to have usually been attached to a related male head of family. Single adult men were also not counted as heads of family.

39. In this study the term Red River settlement includes the parish of Saint-François Xavier and the surrounding White Horse Plains but not the Saulteaux village-Baie St-Paul.

40. The father, Antoine Ducharme, is listed in 1843 as residing in the Saulteaux village with his wife and seven children. With a horse, two mares, an ox and two carts, Antoine was obviously involved in the hunts.

41. The (probable) father, Joseph Desjarlais, is noted as residing in the Saulteaux village in 1840. He is listed as having a wife and 15 children. Eight of these children are less than 16 years of age.

42. François Richard Sr. is listed as residing in the Saulteaux village in 1843. Living with him and his wife were their son and three daughters, all over the age of fifteen. Surprisingly, no animals, carts or other material possession are listed. The census takers only note a house and 2 cultivated acres. Their adult son, Francois Jr., also resided in the Saulteaux village with a wife and three young children. Apparently somewhat well-off, he not only had draft animals (a horse, a mare, an ox, 3 cows and 2 calves) but also possessed 3 carts and cultivated 3 acres.

43. Born in 1825, Abraham McLeod was the son of Antoine Mcleod and an Indian woman who are listed as residing in the Saulteaux village in 1840 and in 1843. They had some draft animals and two carts but cultivated no acreage. Antoine married Cécile Larivière and, from 1859 onward, their children are born in Oak Point.

44. Prior to 1870 the Chaboyers left their home base every year to engage in trading and fishing at Fond du lac. Louis Chaboyer (1801–63) is listed as residing in the Saulteaux village in 1843. Well-to-do, he owned 3 mares, a bull, 2 cows and 2 calves, but no carts or acreage are noted. His wife was Louise Chartrand (born 1820, Saint-Laurent), daughter of Paul Chartrand and Louise Saulteaux. In 1843, they had 5 children all under the age of 16. However, the Chaboyers did not relocate permanently in Saint-Laurent till the 1867–68 famine.

45. He was the son of André Carrière, a French Canadian voyageur from Boucherville, and Angelique Dion, a Métis. The Carrières were an affluent Red River family. For example, in 1840 André, his wife, and 5 children still at home are listed as having a house, a stable, a horse, 5 oxen, 9 cows, 4 calves, 10 pigs, a plough, a harrow, 3 carts, a canoe and cultivating 10 acres! The same year, 25-year-old Louis Carrière, his wife Julie Marchand and 2 young children possessed a house, 2 stables, a mare, an ox, a bull, 2 cows, 2 calves, 3 pigs, a plough, a harrow, 3 carts and cultivated 5 acres. None of the Carrières present in Red River is listed as indigent in the 1868 famine relief census. However, Louis Carrière is found on no lists for that year.

46. Pierre Boyer Jr. (b. 1818) was the son of Pierre Boyer Sr. and Marguerite Bonneau of Grantown. Pierre Boyer Sr. was head of another well-to-do family of Red River. In 1840, he, his wife and seven children possessed a house, a stable, 3 horses, 4 oxen, a bull, 2 cows, 3 calves, a pig, 3 carts and a canoe. They also cultivated 10 acres. Surprisingly, Pierre Boyer Jr., residing in Saint-Laurent with his wife and 6 children, are listed as indigents in the 1868 famine relief census.

47. In the archival records this family's name is capitalized in a variety of ways (Delaronde, DeLaronde, DelaRonde, de la Ronde, etc.). The father of this clan, Louis Delaronde Sr. is found in the Red River censuses for the years 1830, 1831 and 1832. In 1832, Louis Sr., age 29, his wife and 5 young children possessed one house, a horse, a cow, 2 calves, 3 pigs, a canoe and they worked 2 acres. One of the sons, Etienne, would marry Caroline Carrière, daughter of the above-mentioned Louis Carrière.

48. *Le Métis* 2, no. 30, February 22, 1873.

49. The claim process in Saint-Laurent-Oak Point was quite tortuous. The land was resurveyed in 1874 causing several disputes, and in the course of the second land survey several lots previously declared occupied were listed as vacant and vice versa. This served to bury the process even further in a legal quagmire.

50. Of the six Chaboyer households listed in 1868 only two, Antoine Chaboyer, with 5 children below the age of twelve, and "Widow" Chaboyer, with 3 dependents, are listed as being indigents.

51. The "Indian" families noted by Wagner appear not to have been permitted by the Métis to make a claim.

52. D.N. Sprague and R.P. Frye, *The Genealogy of the First Metis Nation* (Winnipeg: Pemmican Publications, 1983), Table 5: "Recognition of Riverlot Occupants by the Government of Canada."

53. Several of the strictly hunting and gathering segments returned seasonally or even remained in the area year round after the transfer. In 1875 the Oblates note that during a retreat:

"The Fathers did not at all expect such crowds of people at the retreat, especially as these poor people have to subsist from day to day by the chase [they came because] They like Father Lacombe because of his knowledge of the Cree language." OMI, AD, L381 M271C, Historical Notes, Parish of Saint-Laurent, 1858–1895.

54. In 1945 there was an investigation of the condition of the "halfbreed" population of Manitoba. In Duck Bay (and Camperville) the residents' names were listed in a census. Those from the Duck Bay-Camperville areas differed completely from those of the Pine Creek Indian Reserve and included many familiar names: Campbell, Chartrand, Delaronde, Lavallée, Pangman and Richard—all of which had been pre-1870 residents of Lake Manitoba. Other names: Flamand, Genaille, Guiboche, Klyne, Lafrenière are listed. Perhaps some of these are from the early hivernants families (Guiboche, for one) who divided their time between fishing, trapping on Lake Winnipegosis and bison hunting in the south-west and simply were never around at census time. PAM, RG 17 B1 Box 90, Natural Resources D.M.'s Files (Preliminary Report for Pine Creek and Duck Bay) 1945.

55. PAM, RG 17, C1#258 1872.

56. OMI, AD, L381 M27C 1, Historical Notes, Parish of Saint-Laurent, page 57.

57. OMI, AD, L381 M27C 1858–1895, Historical Notes, Parish of Saint-Laurent, page 30.

58. Missions de la Congrégation des Missionaires Oblats de Marie Immaculée, Rome, Maison Génerale, 1878. This excerpt is from a letter written by Father Lacombe to the Father General on December 24, 1877.

59. They did not approve really of either the nomadic or trading elements in Saint-Laurent. What they openly dreamed of was a peasant population that engaged in mixed farming with winter fishing as a sideline.

60. Even when pursuing traditional commodity production endeavours, life remained precarious on the south shore: "En ce moment le poisson est bien rare au lac. Plusieurs sont partis pour la Rivière du Chien où ils pêchent sous la glace." AASB, T8170-8173, Camper à Taché, Saint-Laurent, November 24, 1870.

61. In the early years of the mission, secular education was not a high priority for the missionaries partly because of a lack of manpower: "Pour faire l'école à quelques enfants qui ne parlent ni ne comprennent le français pour la plupart; il faudrait sacrifier le soin des âmes." This passage is tantalizing as it indicates, once again, the lack of knowledge of French by the Lake Manitoba Métis, a group that has historically been labelled as "French" Métis. Passages like these, and information extracted during oral history interviews, point to the fact that (some form of) Saulteaux or Cree were the languages

commonly used in the homes. AASB, T9067-T9073, Camper à Taché, Saint-Laurent, July 14, 1871.

62. AASB, T10349, Camper à Taché, Saint-Laurent, May 14, 1872.

63. Pierre Chartrand part demain pour aller faire la chasse du côté de la rivière Poule d'Eau. Il y aurait dit-on du pelu dans ces parages … à la Rivière du Cygne, les gens prennent bien du poisson blanc sous la glace. Quelques-uns des habitants de Saint-Laurent et de la Pointe des Chênes ont pris cette direction. D'autres même sont allés faire la pêche au Poste Manitoba. AASB, T16419, Camper à Taché, Saint-Laurent, automne 1875.

What is not known, and may have made a difference, was if women were actively involved in farm work. They certainly were at a later date. In fact, one key factor in whether or not a family succeeded as dairy farmers was the degree of participation in farm chores of the women. If the wife could keep the farm going while the husband kept cash coming in with his fishing and trapping, their chances of achieving relative affluence and eventual "passing" were greater.

64. One case of infanticide is even discussed in the ecclesiastical correspondence.

65. AASB, T11246–T11249, Camper à Taché, Saint-Laurent, December 1, 1872.

66. AASB, T14595–T14598, Camper à Taché, Saint-Laurent, July 19, see also AASB, T15254–T15257, Camper à Taché, Saint-Laurent, December 28, 1874.

67. *Le Métis*, 1, no. 2, June 8, 1871, "Rapport du Surintendant de l'instruction publique pour les Ecoles Catholiques de la Province du Manitoba (Saint-Laurent). Whether this refusal to learn a new or "foreign" language might be a form of passive resistance learned by children from their "Freemen" parents is unclear.

68. AASB, FD1387–FD1390, Camper à Forget-Despatis, Saint-Laurent, December 11, 1873.

Chapter 3

1. AASB, (T10993), Camper à Taché, Saint-Laurent, October 1, 1872.

2. OMI, AD, L381 M27C 1858–1895, Historical Notes, Parish of Saint-Laurent, page 57. Cécile Larivière seems to have been the daughter of a French Canadian, François, born in Red River Settlement, who apparently had three wives.

3. Peregrinations or "Nomadism" are not the best terms to describe their cycle of displacements since they suggest in common parlance aimless displacements and wanderings. These Métis were following a fairly set seasonal circuit (Saint-Laurent to Duck Bay and return for the most part) within a clearly defined geographical area. These people simply had winter and summer residences.

4. AASB, T10826, Camper à Taché, Saint-Laurent, August 25, 1872. The autumn fishing by Métis and Indians of whitefish for winter provisions remained crucial throughout the 1870s. For a discussion of the paramount importance of fish in the Red River Settlers' diet see: Frank Tough, "'The Storehouses of the Good God': Aboriginal People and Freshwater Fisheries in Manitoba," *Manitoba History* 39 (2000): 2–14.

5. AASB, T15978–T15981, Camper à Taché, Saint-Laurent, May 31, 1875.

6. AASB, T10993, Camper à Taché, Saint-Laurent, October 1, 1872.

7. It is difficult to believe "Rivière du Cygne" refers to the actual Swan River situated 80 km west of Duck Bay overland. They are more likely referring to what was once called Swan Creek which flows into Lake Manitoba 30 km north of Saint-Laurent.

8. AASB, T11117–T11122, Camper à Taché, Saint-Laurent, November 6, 1872.

9. AASB, T15145, Camper à Taché, Saint-Laurent, December 3, 1873.

10. AASB, T16944, Camper à Taché, Saint-Laurent, January 23, 1876.

11. AASB, T16422, Camper à Taché, Saint-Laurent, autumn 1875. This passage is interesting since it indicates that outside of the Duck Bay hivernants and traders, the Saint-Laurent men were leaving their families behind at the mission—labour power for day to day care of any livestock they might have.

12. AASB, T21750–T21753, Camper à Taché, Saint-Laurent, April 28, 1879.

13. AASB, T16419–T16422, Camper à Taché, Saint-Laurent, September 26, 1875.

14. Some of these distinctions predate the 1850s, such as those existing between the trading and hunting-gathering elements of the population.

15. This does not mean the head of the family would not go off for periods of time to hunt or fish, but the family stayed home.

16. It is not clear to what degree the Delarondes were still involved in the fur trade by the 1870s. Father Camper when giving accounts of his trips to Lake Winnipegosis does not mention them except once, in 1876, to comment that St-Math Paul, Joseph Nepinak and their respective families were camping in the old wintering place of Paul and Etienne Laronde at Salt Point (Lake Winnipegosis). AASB, T17239–T17252, Camper à Taché, Saint-Laurent, April 1, 1876.

17. Parish of Saint-Laurent, "Registre destiné à l'enregistrement des Actes de Baptèmes, Mariages et Sépultures de la Paroisse de Saint-Laurent dans le comté de Marquette Est," 1885

18. This is the first of only two indications that some members of this family ever worked for the HBC.

19. AASB, T17239–T17252, Camper à Taché, Saint-Laurent, April 1, 1876.

20. As previously mentioned, sometimes both the "Indian" and the "Métis" wives (and their respective children) were together in the winter encampments. How the women and children really felt about this arrangement is unknown. The priests were certainly scandalised.

21. AASB, T11168–T11171, Lestanc à Taché, Rivière Blanche, February 25, 1873.

22. AASB, T11382–T11389, Camper à Taché, December 26, 1872.

23. AASB, T11168–T11171, Lestanc à Taché, Rivière Blanche, November 13, 1872.

24. AASB, T12250–T12259, Camper à Taché, Saint-Laurent, June 29, 1873.

25. Heather Devine, "Les Desjarlais: The Development and Dispersion of a Proto-Metis Hunting Band, 1785–1870," in Theodore Binnema, Gerhard J. Enns and R.C. Macleod (eds.), *From Rupert's Land to Canada* (Edmonton: University of Alberta Press, 2001), 129–58.

26. Born in Oak Point (1841), he is the son of Joseph Desjarlais and Josette Richard who at one time resided in the Saulteaux village.

27. For a fascinating glimpse at this segment of the population, listen to PAM, Métis Oral History Project (hereafter MOHP) 1984, C342, C343, C344.

28. *Les Cloches de Saint-Boniface* (hereafter LCSB), vol. 5, 1906, page 194.

29. The general lifestyles, habits and worldview of these people make one think of the descriptions given by Slabodin of the Mackenzie District Métis rather than the typical Red River Métis. Please consult: Richard Slobodin, *Métis of the Mackenzie District* (Ottawa: Resource Centre for Anthropological Research, St. Paul University, 1966).

30. LCSB, vol. 5, 1906, page 194. This trend probably started in the late 1860s, please refer to: AASB, T5499–T5502, Camper à Taché, Saint-Laurent, April 23, 1868. Of course a majority of the families in Saint-Laurent were more comfortable speaking Saulteaux or Cree as opposed to French in the 1870s but, as previously argued, they still maintained a distinction between themselves and those they considered to be "Indian." Assimilation appears to have occurred in the north, except in places like Duck Bay where the Métis migration, post-1870, was significant, and where the hivernants resided yearly in quite large numbers up till the 1890s. Even today residents of Duck Bay and Camperville consider themselves to be "distinct" from the reserve dwellers.

12. This municipality included the settlements of Saint-Laurent and Oak Point and all the land to the east that had been given out in halfbreed scrip (townships 16–17). Its boundaries were increased between 1881 and 1891. Outside the two settlements the municipality was almost completely unoccupied, as most of the scrip belonged to speculators.

32. Missions des Oblats de Marie Immaculée, 1887, pages 150–51.

33. *North-West Free Press*, November 23, 1881, page 3.

34. Numbers of farming animals would fluctuate wildly from year to year and from season to season depending on the amount and quality of hay available, the success of winter fishing (no need to slaughter extra animals for food), the prices given for fur, seneca root, etc.

35. Manitoba, Department of Agriculture, Report of the Department of Agriculture and Statistics for the Province of Manitoba, 1880, page 88; 1882, page 62. Saint-Laurent Municipality, Tax Assessment Roll 1883, quoted in Richtik, "Historical Geography," 50. Unfortunately, it appears most pre-WWII documents have disappeared from the municipal offices of Saint-Laurent in the interval between 1964 and 1989 when initial research for this project was done. Efforts at locating the Tax Rolls through conversations with Dr. Richtik, Municipal Affairs (Wnp) and research at the PAM proved fruitless.

36. PAM, 1881 Census, C13283–186-L (Marquette, Woodlands, Municipality of Saint-Laurent).

37. PAM, 1881 Census, C13284–186-5 (extensions) D (Northeast-Lake Winnipegosis). The last day for the lake Winnipegosis was October 3, 1881. This is still quite early for the hivernants to make their way to Duck Bay.

38. He was remarried to Louise Ducharme sometime between 1891 and 1894.

39. Mercier, *Renseignements sur Saint-Laurent, Manitoba*, 42.

40. His first official wife, Geneviève Robert, was no longer mentioned by this time.

41. University of Manitoba's Department of Agriculture "hotline" provided the statistic of 15 bushels of seed potatoes required to plant one acre.

42. Guy Lavallée, in his ethnography on Saint-Laurent comments that it was common for newlyweds to live with either the groom or bride's parents till one or two children had been born. This would have allowed for a certain amount of work specialisation within the household economy. However, it is difficult to determine if this residency pattern is only a 20th-century phenomenon or if it was the custom among 19th-century Lake Manitoba Métis. Guy Lavallée, "The Métis People of St.Laurent, Manitoba: An Introductory Ethnography" (MA thesis, Department of Anthropology, University of British Columbia), 63–64.

43. Being near the water and at a point of transit, they may have been builders of the oft-mentioned "barges" (large flat bottom boats that used both oars and sails).

44. As stated previously, the Chaboyers claimed the greatest number of river lots in 1872 (6).

45. PAM, RG17 D2, river lot files (Lot 15), Parish of Saint-Laurent

46. This would have given them a yearly crop averaging 320 bushels of potatoes. Both came from well-to-do Red River families. Pierre Boyer's father, Pierre senior, was listed in 1843 as owning several oxen and horses, cultivating 12 acres in Saint-François Xavier and owning 6 carts. Genevieve's Father, Abraham Martin, also owned several draft animals, cultivated 18 acres in Saint-François Xavier and possessed 7 carts.

47. Pierre Boyer's grandson stated in an interview taped in 1987 that his family came up during "la grande misère." MLC, 1987, tape 9, sides 1 and 2.

48. Giraud, *Le Métis Canadien,* 752. This Louis Guiboche is found in the Red River censuses from 1827 to 1835. Well-to-do, in 1835 for example, he is listed, with his wife and six young children, as occupying a house and owning a stable, barn, 5 horses, 4 oxen, a bull, 4 cows, 2 calves, 6 pigs, a plough, a harrow, 4 carts, a boat, a canoe and cultivating 12 acres in Red River.

49. MLC, 1987, Tapes no. 14–15, Tape 15 side 2.

50. Mercier, *Renseignements sur Saint-Laurent, Manitoba,* 10.

51. In the 1881 census there are at least three Pierre Chartrands listed (two in Winnipegosis and one in the Saint-Laurent/Duck Bay area). It is possible that one of them is counted twice, given the months elapsed and the highly mobile nature of that family, but it is as likely that such a large clan would have had several members with the same first name.

52. Mercier, *Renseignements sur Saint-Laurent, Manitoba,* 13.

53. Since the Chaboyers had been involved in some sort of trading activity in the 1860s at La Mission, it is not really surprising they would extend northward after their permanent move to Saint-Laurent in 1867–68. In the 1870s and 1880s the fur trade frontier was receding northward and hunting and gathering Métis were no longer passing through Saint-Laurent on their way to bison hunting grounds. Fur trade peddlers would have to make their way north. The Chaboyer listed in the summer of 1881 as being a trader in Saint-Laurent may have been more interested in the buying and selling of dried fish rather than pelts.

54. Term (coined c. 1863) used, especially in the United States, to describe marriage or sexual relations between a man and a woman of different races.

Chapter 4

1. "Étranges"–strange (as opposed to "étrangers"–strangers) was the term used by the local Saint-Laurent inhabitants to designate the newly arrived immigrants.

2. It should always be kept in mind that any number of Métis families who viewed this area as their home base might be missing from a particular census. Many continued the habit of going north to hunt, fish, trade, or visit at different times of the year.

3. AASB, T23847–T234849, Camper à Taché, Saint-Laurent, May 17, 1880.

4. OMI, AD, L381 M27C 1, 1858–1895, Historical Notes, Parish of Saint-Laurent, page 71.

5. Donatien Frémont, *Les Français dans l'Ouest Canadien,* Vol. 1 (Saint-Boniface: Éditions du Blé, 1980), 11. The 1891 census lists Ovide Lacoursiere (age 58) as being a "manager of ranch and cheese factory." Living with him were his wife Virginie (age 55); "Louis Recour" (age 13); "Napoleon and Mary Rivard" (farm labourers, both age 30) and their infants Joseph and Mary (ages 1). Except for the infants, all were born in the province of Quebec.

6. Saint-Laurent municipality, Tax Assessment Rolls 1891, quoted in Richtik, "Historical Geography."

7. Charles De Simencourt, age 36, is listed in 1891 as being a farmer; born in England, of a French-born father and an English-born mother. His wife Clara, age 30, was of English-born parents. They had one son Charles, age 2, born in Manitoba.

8. *Le Métis* 13, no. 13, November 15, 1883, page 3.

9. *Le Métis* 12, no. 20, February 26, 1885, page 12.

10. In 1881, a public highway was built, crossing the municipality from Oak Point to Winnipeg. This would have been an improvement over the old fur-trade cart trail that existed previously, allowing for the easier shipment of goods and livestock. OMI, AD, L381 M27C 1, Historical Notes, Parish of Saint-Laurent, page 48.

11. Frémont, *Les Français dans l'Ouest Canadien*, 1.

12. AASB, T46275, Camper à Taché, Saint-Laurent, January 10, 1892.

13. In the 1891 census "Ernest Trudel" (age 38) is listed as a literate farm labourer originating from Quebec. He and his wife, "Georgena" (age 36), had 7 children. The first five were born in Quebec the last two in Manitoba.

14. Pervasive illiteracy within the Métis adult population also may have been an obstacle in mounting a successful business.

15. "The general dependence on cattle is not surprising, for the municipality was too far from the railway for convenient shipment of grain, and it had abundant grass lands for grazing and hay production and soils ill suited to grain growing. Animal and animal product were the only source of farm income; crops were grown for farm use." Richtik, "Historical Geography," 121.

16. *Le Métis* 18, no. 23, March 28, 1889, page 3. Sigfroid and Sophie Lachance came from Quebec with eight children in the early 1880s. By 1891, their oldest son, Joseph (age 22), was also listed as a farmer. Interestingly, this family would eventually relocate to Baie St-Paul/Saint-Eustache where land was much more fertile. Also, a branch of the family would head towards the parish of San Clara, near the Saskatchewan border, where former impoverished Baie Saint Paul Métis were also relocating in the opening decades of the 20th century. In both places they became successful farmers.

17. Wood moulds that contained approximately one pound of butter.

18. AASB, T35087–T35088, Camper à Taché, Saint-Laurent, January 9, 1887.

19. Les Missions Oblates de Marie Immaculée (1881), 349.

20. "Un parti nous a quitté avec 14 chevaux. Ils se rend à Fairford à 130 miles d'ici pour acheter du poisson." *Le Métis* 13, no. 9, December 13, 1889, page 3.

21. *Le Métis* 12, no. 20, February 26, 1885, page 3.

22. *Le Métis* 12, no. 13, January 17, 1883, page 3.

23. *Le Métis* 13, no.21, March 13, 1884, page 4.

24. Explaining why so many families are absent from the census list.

25. Obviously the farming families would not be able to displace themselves in such a manner.

26. AASB, T52856–T52863, Camper à Taché, Saint-Laurent, April 18, 1881.

27. Ibid.

28. Ibid., October 30, 1882.

29. *Le Métis* 15, no. 51, October 6, 1887, page 3.

30. AASB, T25659–T25662, Camper à Taché, Saint-Laurent, June 28, 1881.

31. OMI, AD, L381 M27C 2, Historical Notes, Parish of Saint-Laurent, 1896–1899.

32. AASB, T26637–T26639, Camper à Taché, Saint-Laurent, May 9, 1882.

33. AASB, T52856–T52863, Camper à Taché, Saint-Laurent, April 18, 1881.

34. AASB, T23618–T23625, Camper à Taché, Saint-Laurent, April 8, 1880.

35. During the 1880s most Métis seem to have left Oak Point. There is no data to suggest that any of the Métis in Oak Point received patent for the land they occupied. In 1882 Camper would comment, "Deux familles, Johny Loyer et Antoine Desjarlais viennent s'établir à la mission … il ne reste plus grand monde à la Pointe des Chênes." AASB, T26708–T26711, Camper à Taché, Saint-Laurent, June 2, 1882.

36. AASB, T29065-T29074, Camper à Taché, Saint-Laurent, April 4, 1884.

37. AASB, T30386–T30389, Camper à Taché, Saint-Laurent, December 10, 1884.

38. AASB, T28514–T28519, Camper à McColl, Saint-Laurent, December 29, 1883.

39. Probably a reference to the old *Hommes Libres* designation for the hunting and gathering Métis population who had not resided in the Red River Settlement prior to 1870.

40. AASB, T28592–T28595, Camper à Taché, Saint-Laurent, January 2, 1884.

41. AASB, L46101–L46102, Camper à Langevin, Saint-Laurent, February 8, 1901.

42. "M. Hanover de Winnipeg est venu faire sa deuxième moisson de pelleteries. Quoique le produit de cette année sous ce rapport soit inférieur à celui des années passées les marchands se déclarent assez satisfait." *Le Métis* 20, no. 19, February 18, 1891, page 3.

43. Canada, Parliament, "Report of the Department of Indian Affairs," *Sessional Papers*, 1893, Paper no. 14, page 56.

44. One such freighter is Jean Delaronde (John Laronde). After the mid-1880s his name is no longer mentioned in the ecclesiastical correspondence.

45. Donald Gunn, "Notes."

46. AASB, T27159–T27161, Camper à Taché, Saint-Laurent, October 30, 1882.

47. Richtik, "Historical Geography," 93.

48. P.R. Mailhot, "Ritchot's Resistance: Abbé Noel Joseph Ritchot and the Creation and the transformation of Manitoba" (Ph.D dissertation, University of Manitoba, 1988), 238–54.

49. N. St-Onge, "Métis and Merchant Capital in Red River, the Dissolution of Pointe à Grouette 1860–1885" (MA thesis, University of Manitoba, 1983), 125–28.

50. Mercier, *Renseignements sur Saint-Laurent, Manitoba,* 13.

51. One Sayer family is listed in the Saint-Laurent area for the 1881 census. William, a hunter, and his wife Larose Sayer (ages 25 and 17) are listed along with their 2 daughters Sarah (2) and Virginie (3).

52. This discrepancy in the reporting of age is the norm rather than the exception in all the censuses and church records. How a Métis felt when the question of age was posed to him seems as important as the actual passing of years in the determining a number.

53. "Le jeune Pierre Chartrand est mort vendredi matin entre 4 et 5 heures… Vous ne saurez croire tout le vide que cette mort fait dans notre pauvre petite paroisse. Il avait affaire avec tout le monde et faisait vivre et soulageait tant de monde." *The young Pierre Chartrand died Friday morning between 4 and 5 o'clock… You would not believe the effect this death has on our little parish. He had dealings with everyone and helped many people get by.* AASB, T34641–T34644, Camper à Taché, Saint-Laurent, October 31, 1886.

54. By 1901 Elise Chartrand (née Delaronde) had remarried with John Guiboche, described as a "peddler" in the census.

55. AASB, L6336–L6340, Camper à Taché, Saint-Laurent, October 19, 1896.

56. The 1891 census for the Duck Bay area was not found.

57. Most sources state his wife to be Philomène Laronde (b. 1858), daughter of Etienne and Caroline (Carrière) Laronde.

58. It is in this context that an analysis of the 1883, 1891, and 1902 Saint-Laurent Tax Assessment Rolls would have been valuable. They would have given a household by household breakdown of the acreage owned, acreage cultivated, buildings, size of livestock herd, etc. Unfortunately, between 1964 and 1989 these documents disappeared from the Saint-Laurent municipal offices.

59. AASB, T44726–T44728, Camper à Taché, Saint-Laurent, May 5, 1891.

60. Father Camper received a patent for a portion of that lot on December 2, 1881. PAM, RG17 D2, Parish River Lot Files, Parish of Saint-Laurent (information found in file discussing lot 10).

61. AASB, T26633–T26634, Camper à Taché, Saint-Laurent, May 1, 1882.

62. Richtik ("Historical Geography," 51) notes, without giving his source, that there were cattle feeding stations in the Mary Hill in the 1870s.

63. MLC, 1987, Tape no 9, side 1.

64. They were the children of Louis Laronde and Judith Morin.

65. AASB, T52856–T52863, Camper à Taché, Saint-Laurent, 18 April 1881.

66. Her "lodgers" were Agnes (Laronde) (age 12); Jules Petregum (age 26), her domestic and farm labourer from France, with his Manitoba born wife "Margaret" (age 21) and their daughter Mary (age 2).

67. He was the son of Alexis Carrière and Suzanne Ducharme.

68. MLC, 1987, Tape 9, side 2. Yet the 1901 enumerator, William Logan, listed Elzear and Marie Anne Boyer as being both "Cree half-breeds" and "farmers." Most French-speaking, Manitoba-born heads of family in Saint-Laurent were listed as Halfbreeds. How they were coming to perceive themselves and how the English-speaking Protestant outside world saw them appear to be two different things.

69. MLC, 1987, tape no 37, side 1.

70. The origins of this family are nebulous.

71. Published genealogies indicate he was married to Anne Fiddler (born 1861) and had one child by her in 1864 at Fort Ellice named Pierre. The 1891 census lists 38-year-old "Philomena" (born in the North-West) as his wife. Four children are listed, with "Pierre" being the eldest. It is possible Roger Nabase's first wife was deceased, and as was the custom, he rapidly remarried.

72. "Un des Campbell du Poste Manitoba veut s'établir à la mission avec toute la famille. Il a quatre enfants. Il est arrivé ces jours derniers avec armes et baggages." AASB, T23618–T23625, Saint-Laurent, Camper à Taché, April 8, 1880.

73. Of course we only know of families who were physically present to be counted up in the spring of 1891. From the correspondence of the Oblates it is evident there were hunting and gathering families, some, most probably from the north, who were residing for various parts of the year in Saint-Laurent. They peopled the previously mentioned fringe settlement of Fort Rouge. Most of these people were still in their wintering camps or away muskrat hunting in April–May of 1891.

74. MLC, 1987, Tape 3, side 1.

75. A daughter, in the course of an Oral History interview, confirmed Alfred Klyne's 1891 statement that he is a carpenter. MLC, 1987, tape no 4, side 1.

76. Pierre Daniel Coutu (b. Saint-Boniface 1863) and Alexandre Norbert Coutu (b. Saint-Boniface 1867) were the sons of Pierre Henri Coutu (b. 1835 Berthierville, Quebec) and Marie-Catherine Lagimodière.

77. *Le Métis* 21, no. 1, October 14, 1891, page 3.

78. *Le Métis* 23, no. 25, March 29, 1894, page 3.

79. Also spelled Laurence.

80. Their brother Didgime Laurence would join them in Saint-Laurent and work as a farm labourer.

81. A Winnipeg to Oak Point line was completed in 1904. Mercier, *Renseignements sur Saint-Laurent, Manitoba,* 15 (English text).

82. MLC, 1987, tape no 7, side 1.

83. PAM, MOHP, 1984, C346. Interestingly, Charles Lambert was listed in the 1901 census as a "Chippewa Halfbreed." His wife was a "Cree Halfbreed."

84. This fact complicates any attempt to evaluate the importance of trading as an economic activity for Saint-Laurent. The 1891 census takers began their work on April 6, 1891. At that time the lake would still be frozen solid. Traders working in the north would still be, like the hivernants, in their winter quarters. On April 25, 1906 Brother Mulvihill made the comment that "The ice on the lake broke up today and is now moving ... this is the earliest in 30 years!"

85. The correlation between date of arrival and social and economic position is only partial. Some pre-1870 individuals, such as Michel Chartrand or Pierre Chaboyer, became and remained quite successful. Also, there are indications that Fort Rouge inhabitants trickled in (and out) well into the 20th century. But, as a group, those families arriving after c. 1880 that are found in the census are by far the most "successful."

86. One should keep in mind that some of these southern "farming" families might have been in Saint-Laurent for just a season. Camper in a letter written in 1891, noted: "En 1890 le nombre de communions pascales pour Saint-Laurent a été beaucoup plus considerable que de coutume à cause des hivernants venus de différentes paroisses." In 1890 the number of Easter communions in Saint-Laurent increased sharply because of all the winterers who have come from various parishes. AASB, T44726–T44728, Camper à Taché, Saint-Laurent, May 5, 1891. One of the reasons these people wintered in the area was to cash in on high fish prices; "la petite rivière nous fait l'effet d'un marché tant sont nombreux les camps de pêcheurs qui accourent de tous les côtés." *Le Métis* 13, no. 21, March 13, 1884, page 3.

87. Richtik makes the comment that as late as 1883 land outside the river lots was still largely in the hands of speculators. He bases his observation on data contained in the tax assessment rolls for 1883.

Chapter 5

1. Canada, Bureau of Statistics, Census of Canada, volume 1.

2. Madeleine L. Proctor, *Woodland Echoes* (Steinbach, MB: Derksen Printers, 1960), 140.

3. This does not include members of the Catholic Church such as the Oblate fathers and brothers and members of the order of Franciscan nuns that taught at the local convent.

4. *Le Métis* 24, no. 17, March 13, 1895, page 3.

5. *Le Métis* 24, no. 23, April 24, 1895, page 3.

6. One should remember that, even prior to 1860, there already existed in Fond du Lac two distinct socio-economic groups: the four trading clans and the hunting and gathering families.

7. PAM, MOHP, 1984, C341, C352, C349, C357.

8. PAM, MOHP, 1984, C353.

9. Napoleon Chartrand, a teacher in the 1891 census, is now the only official cheese maker in Saint-Laurent. He is listed as being an employee but his wages are not noted.

10. Michel Chartrand, now with his second wife Louise Ducharme, would be the only known Chartrand to pursue this family's time-honoured occupation of "merchant" in 1901. Michel had declared this occupation in 1881, but in 1891 he had described himself a "farmer." This man stated he could both read and write French but not English, and that his mother tongue was Cree.

11. AASB L56120, Paroisse de Saint-Laurent recensement 28 novembre 1910 (H. Peran, OMI).

12. Daughter of Antoine Chartrand and Françoise Makons–sauteuse.

13. In 1907 he would marry Alice Josephine Gaudry.

14. He was the son of Jean Baptiste Lagimodière and Marie Anne Gaboury. His daughter was Marie Anne Lagimodière (or Lagimoniere), deceased wife of Pierre Henry Coutu.

15. OMI, AD, L111 M27C, Rapport du Vicaire des Missions de Saint-Boniface, 1893, page 9. *Missions Oblates de Marie Immaculée* (Rome: Maison Générale, 1898), 281; (1907): 327–29.

16. *Missions des Oblats de Marie Immaculée*, 1927, page 341.

17. AASB, L56120, Paroisse de Saint-Laurent, Manitoba, novembre 28, 1910 (recensement paroissial).

18. LCSB, vol. 10, no. 5, 1 March 1911, page 64. "Not one took out a homestead; all prefer to buy land to their taste and be immediately masters in their own home."

19. Ibid., pages 64–66.

20. Ibid.

21. Two of these families, John and Rose Connelley (Connelly) and Cornelius and Annie Connelley, were already well-established farming and ranching families in 1901. That year, between the two couples there were 18 living children. The Connellys began to appear in the Saint-Laurent censuses in 1891. That year, John Connelly was managing a cattle ranch and Cornelius Connelly was described as a farmer.

22. There is no clear indication that they ever received letters patent to their river lots.

23. Saint-Laurent Municipality, Tax Assessment Roll 1911, quoted in Richtik, "Historical Geography," 201.

24. Lay and church authorities were by and large the same group. One had to be a "good" Catholic to be a municipal councillor or a school trustee.

25. AASB, L5140–L5143, Camper à Langevin, Saint-Laurent, May 21, 1896.

26. *Missions des Oblats de Marie Immaculée*, 1907, 326.

27. *Giraud, Le Métis Canadien*, 1271–72 (italics added). Still in the 1910 parish census, the children of the seven mixed marriages (Métis and non-Métis spouse) would be labelled "Métis" by the parish priest.

28. In 1984 an interviewee, when asked to list the big farmers of her youth (1920s), listed, along with typically Breton names, the Chartrand, Lavallée, Carrière, and the Gaudry families. The Gaudry are a Métis family originating from Lorette, Manitoba. They seem to have moved to the Saint-Laurent area after 1891. André Gaudry Sr. had a farm five miles south of the Church in the early 1900s and, according to a daughter-in-law, had "lots" of cows and horses.

29. F.H. Leacy (ed.), *Historical Statistics of Canada* (Ottawa: Statistics Canada, 1983), section M.

30. After 1911 most rural cheese factories closed down as cream could be shipped directly to Winnipeg and processed there more cheaply. Saint-Laurent farmers could count on a daily freight train to carry their goods south.

31. This connection with Chicago had begun in the 1880s. *Le Métis* 13, no. 21, March 13, 1884.

32. AASB, T30260–T30263, Camper à Taché, Saint-Laurent, November 12, 1884.

33. Russ Rothney and Steve Watson, *Brief Economic History of Northern Manitoba* (Northern Planning Exercise, July 1975), 153.

34. PAM, MOHP, 1984, C349.

35. Rothney and Watson, *A Brief Economic History of Northern Manitoba*, 41.

36. Ibid., 57.

37. OMI, AD, L381 M27R9, Historical Notes, Parish of Saint-Laurent, page 58.

38. Rothney and Watson, *Brief Economic History of Northern Manitoba*, 46.

39. Ibid.

40. Lagassé, *People of Indian Ancestry in Manitoba*, vol. 3, 67–70.

41. F.H. Leacy, *Historical Statistics of Canada*, section N.

42. PAM, MOHP, 1984, C353.

43. AD, OMI, L381 M27R 9, pages 2–4. In this document the poor segment of the population is labelled "Métis" but the writer is quick to point out that there are families of Métis descent who are now "good" families fully capable of meeting these higher financial obligations.

44. AD, OMI, L381 M27R 9, pages 2–4.

45. PAM, MOHP, 1984, C351–2, C356, C360. For a contrasting view on the clergy listen to C342–344.

46. Lagassé, *People of Indian Ancestry in Manitoba*, vol. 1, 72.

47. PAM, MOHP, 1984, C342–3, C351–2, C357, C363, C364.

48. MLC, 1987, tapes no. 24 and 25.

49. MLC, 1987, tape no 35, side 1.

50. PAM, MOHP, 1984, Interviews C342–3, C351–2, C357, C363, C364.

51. *Missions des Oblats de Marie Immaculée*, 1920, page 273.

52. OMI, AD, L381 M27R9.

53. Ibid.

54. PAM, MOHP, 1984, C351–2. For an interesting but clearly biased description of typical Fort Rouge inhabitants read the *Mission des Oblats de Marie Immaculée*, 1901, pages 85–98.

55. Walter Hlady commented in a draft version of vol.3 of the Lagassé report that "Métis" attitudes toward gardening were conditioned by their subsistence activities: "For many the necessity to go out harvesting the seneca root, fishing, cutting pulpwood and taking casual employment, all of which usually meant leaving the home community for extended periods, was a valid reason for not gardening."

56. For an interesting discussion on fish prices for the lake Winnipeg fishermen see interview PAM, MOHP, 1985, C383.

57. PAM, MOHP, 1984–85, C357, C363, C385.

58. Great Slave Lake remains the site of the largest commercial fishing enterprise in the Mackenzie District and the only one heavily involving Métis. Many are what anthropologist Richard Slabodin defines as (inaccurately, I believe) "'Red River' Métis: A broad category taking in families that trace their roots to the pre-1870 fur trade era. Many went up at the turn of the century and later from the northern prairies where they already had engaged in commercial fishing. Métis from almost every western province are represented among those holding commercial fishing licenses at Hay River. To this day commercial fishing is a major occupation of 'Red River' Métis not only at Great Slave Lake but also at the older established fisheries in Saskatchewan and Alberta, at Lesser Slave, Athabasca, Wollaston, and Reindeer Lakes." Richard Slabodin, "Subarctic Métis," *Subarctic*, Handbook of North American Indians series, Washington: Smithsonian Institution, 1981, 368–69.

59. *Le Métis* 22, no. 32, 1893, page 3.

60. PAM, MOHP, 1984–85 (description of father's occupation).

61. Rothney and Watson, *Brief Economic History of Northern Manitoba*, 57.

62. Lagassé, *People of Indian Ancestry in Manitoba*, vol. 3, 77–86.

Conclusion

1. Quoted above.

2. Robert Miles, "Class, Race and Ethnicity: A Critique of Cox's Theory," *Ethnic and Racial Studies* 3, no. 2 (April 1980).

3. They may have gone to lay a claim to their land at the Dominion Lands Office and been verbally dissuaded to do so (due to a lack of "improvements").

4. AASB, T35087–T35088 Passim, Camper à Taché, Saint-Laurent, January 9, 1887.

5. P.R. Mailhot and D N. Sprague, "Persistent Settlers: The Dispersal and Resettlement of the Red River Metis, 1870–1885," *Canadian Journal of Ethnic Studies* 17 (1985).

6. Lagassé, *People of Indian Ancestry in Manitoba*, 77.

Bibliography

Consulted Works

I. Primary Sources

A. Archival Collections

1. National Archives of Canada

Association de la Propagation de la Foi–Paris

2. Provincial Archives of Manitoba

Manitoba Census of 1870; Manitoba Census of 1881; Manitoba Census of 1891; Manitoba Census of 1901; Métis Oral History Project; Minute Book of the Executive Relief Committee 1868-69; Natural Resources D.M.'s Files; Parish Lot Files–Oak Point; Parish Lot Files–Saint-Laurent; Red River Relief Committee–Statistical Reports 1968; Register of Surveyor Returns; Surveyor's Field Notes; Vital Statistics, Parish Register of Saint-Laurent, 1864-1883

3. Archives de l'Archevêché de Saint-Boniface (Centre du Patrimoine)

Fonds Provencher; Fonds Taché; G.A. Belcourt correspondence; Joseph Camper correspondence; Ambroise C. Comeau correspondence; Zephirin Gascon correspondence; Jean-Marie Lestanc correspondence; Joseph McCarthy correspondence; Jérémie Mulvihill correspondence; Hervé Peran correspondence; Jean-Baptiste Proulx correspondence; Laurent Simonet correspondence

4. Hudson's Bay Company Archives

Post Journals–(Fort Garry Journal–B.235/a/9); Reports and correspondence of Sir George Simpson (D4/1 to D4/110), (D5/1 to D5/52)

5. Archives Deschâtelets (Oblats de Marie Immaculée)

Collection paroisse Abbéville, Manitoba; Collection paroisse de Sainte-Claire, Manitoba; Collection paroisse de Saint-Laurent, Manitoba; Rapport du Vicaire des Missions de Saint-Boniface (1893)

6. Department of Native Studies, University of Manitoba

Michif Language Committee–Oral History Collection

7. Parish of Saint-Laurent

Parish Register–1885

B. Published Documents

Begg, Alexander. 1894–95. *History of the North West*. 3 vols. Toronto: Rose and Company.

Bryce, George. 1887. *A Short History of the Canadian People*. London.

Campbell, Maria. 1973. *Halfbreed*. Toronto: McLelland and Stewart.

Canada. Bureau of Statistics, *Census of Canada*, Volume 1.

——. 1893. "Report of the Department of Indian Affairs." *Sessional Papers*.

Gunn, Donald. 1872. "Notes of an Egging Expedition to Shoal Lake, West of Lake

Winnipeg." Annual Report of the Board of Regents of the Smithsonian Institution for the Year 1867. Washington: Government Printers.

Hind, Henry Youle. 1860. *Narrative of the Canadian Red River Exploring Expedition of 1857 and of the Assiniboine and Saskatchewan Exploring Expedition of 1858.* London: Longman, Green, Langman and Roberts.

Leary, F.H. (ed.). 1983. *Historical Statistics of Canada.* 2nd ed. Ottawa: Statistics Canada.

Manitoba. 1880, 1882. Department of Agriculture. *Report of the Department of Agriculture and Statistics for the Province of Manitoba.*

Morice, A.G. 1908. *Dictionnaire des Canadiens et Métis Français de l'Ouest.* Saint-Boniface: Chez l'Auteur.

Morin, Gail. 1998. *Censuses of the Red River Settlement.* Pawtucket, RI: Quintin Publications.

———. 2001. *Metis Families: A Genealogical Compendium,* 6 volumes. 2nd ed. Pawtucket, RI: Quintin Publications.

Nute, G.L. (ed.). 1942. *Documents Relating to the North West Missions, 1815–1827.* St. Paul: Minnesota Historical Society.

Sprague, D.N. and R.P. Frye. 1983. *The Genealogy of the First Métis Nation: The Development and Dispersal of the Red River Settlement, 1820–1900.* Winnipeg: Pemmican Books.

C. Newspapers

Les Cloches de Saint-Boniface; *Le Métis* (Saint-Boniface); *Missions de la Congrégation des Missionaires Oblats de Marie Immaculée* (Paris); *North-West Free Press* (Winnipeg);

II. Secondary Sources

A. General Works

Baldwin, Stuart. 1980. "Wintering Villages of the Metis Hivernant: Documentary and Archaeological Evidence." Photocopied

Bourgeault, Ron. 1983. "The Indian, the Métis and Fur Trade, Class, Sexism and Racism in the Transition from Communism to Capitalism." *Studies in Political Economy* 12 (Fall).

Brown, Jennifer S.H.. 1980. *Strangers in Blood: Fur Trade Company Families in Indian Country.* Vancouver: University of Columbia Press.

———. 1994. "Fur Trade as Centrifuge: Familial Dispersal and Offspring Identity in Two Company Contexts." Pp. 197–219 in Raymond J. DeMallie and Alfonso Ortiz (eds.), *North American Indian Anthropology: Essays on Society and Culture.* Norman: University of Oklahoma Press.

Bumsted, J.M.. 1999. *Fur Trade Wars: the Founding of Western Canada.* Winnipeg: Great Plains Publications.

Burley, David V., Gayel A. Horsfall and John D. Brandon. 1992. *Structural Considerations of Metis Ethnicity: An Archaeological, Architectural, and Historical Study.* Vermillion SD: University of South Dakota Press.

Carrière, G. 1979. "The Early Efforts of the Oblate Missionaries in Western Canada." *Prairie Forum* 4.

Cornell, Paul G. et al. 1971. *Canada Unité et Diversité.* Toronto: Holt Rinehart and Winston.

Cowie, Isaac. 1913. *The Company of Adventurers: A Narrative of Seven Years in the Service of the Hudson's Bay Company During 1867–1874 on the Great Buffalo Plains.* Toronto: William Briggs.

Creighton, D.G. 1955. *Sir John A. Macdonald.* Vol. 2, *The Old Chieftain.* Toronto: University of Toronto Press.

Devine, Heather. 2001. "Les Desjarlais : The Development and Dispersion of a Proto-Metis Hunting Band, 1785-1870." Pp. 129–58 in Theodore Binnema, Gerhard J. Enns and R.C. Macleod (eds.), *From Rupert's Land to Canada.* Edmonton: University of Alberta Press.

Doll, Maurice F.V., Robert S. Kidd and John P. Day. 1988. *The Buffalo Lake Metis Site: A Late Nineteenth Century Settlement in the Parkland of Central Alberta* (Occasional Paper No. 4). Edmonton: Alberta Culture and Multiculturalism Historical Resources Division.

Douaud, Patrick. 1985. *Ethnolinguistic Profile of the Canadian Métis.* Ottawa: Canada National Museum of Man.

Drieken, Paul. 1985. *We Are Métis: The Ethnography of a Halfbreed Community in Northern Alberta.* New York: AMS Press.

Dugas, Abbé G. 1889. *Monseigneur Provencher et les Missions de la Rivière-Rouge.* Montréal: C. O. Beauchemin et Fils.

Dusenberry, Verne. 1985. "Waiting for a Day That Never Comes: The Dispossessed Métis of Montana." Pp. 119–36 in J. Brown and J. Peterson (eds.), *The New Peoples: Being and Becoming Métis in North America.* Winnipeg: University of Manitoba Press.

Ens, Gerhard. 1989. "Dispossession or Adaption? Migration or Persistence of the Red River Métis, 1835–1890." *Historical Papers 1988 Communications Historiques.* Ottawa.

——. 1996. *Homeland to Hinterland: The Changing Worlds of the Red River Metis in the Nineteenth Century.* Toronto: Toronto University Press.

——. 2001. "Metis Ethnicity, Personal Identity and the Development of Capitalism in the Western Interior: the Case of Johnny Grant." Pp. 161–77 in Theodore Binnema, Gerhard J. Enns and R.C. Macleod (eds.), *From Rupert's Land to Canada.* Edmonton: University of Alberta Press.

Flanaghan, Thomas (ed.). 1976. *The Diaries of Louis Riel.* Edmonton: Hurtig Publishers.

——. 1976. *Louis "David" Riel: Prophet of the New World.* Toronto: University of Toronto Press.

Foster, John E. 1985. "Some Questions and Perspectives on the Problem of Métis Roots." Pp. 73–91 in J. Brown and J. Peterson (eds.), *The New Peoples: Being and Becoming Métis in North America.* Winnipeg: University of Manitoba Press.

——. 1986. "The Plains Métis." Pp. 388–94 in R. Bruce Morrison and C. Roderick Wilson (eds.), *Natives Peoples: The Canadian Experience,* 2nd ed. Toronto: McClelland & Stewart.

——. 2001. "Wintering, the Outsider Adult Male and the Ethnogenesis of the WesternPlains Metis." Pp. 179–91 in Theodore Binnema, Gerhard J. Enns and R.C. Macleod (eds.), *From Rupert's Land to Canada.* Edmonton: University of Alberta Press.

Fremont, Donatien. 1980. *Les Français dans l'Ouest Canadien.* Saint-Boniface: Editions du Blé.

Friesen, Gerald. 1984. *The Canadian Prairies: A History.* Toronto: University of Toronto Press.

Giraud, Marcel. 1945. *Le Métis Canadien.* Paris: Institut d'Ethnologie.

Gupta, Dipankar. 1983. "Racism Without Color: The Catholic Ethic and Ethnicity in Québec." *Race and Class* 25, no. 1.

Hamilton, Scott and B.A. Nicholson. 2000. "Metis Land Use of the Lauder Sandhills of Southwestern Manitoba." *Prairie Forum* 2 (Fall): 243–70.

Howard, Joseph. 1952. *Strange Empire: Louis Riel and the First Métis People.* Toronto: James Lewis and Samuel.

Huel, Raymond J.A.. 1996. *Proclaiming the Gospel to the Indians and the Métis*. Edmonton: University of Alberta Press.

Innis, Harold. 1962. *The Fur Trade in Canada*. 2nd ed. Toronto: University of Toronto Press.

Lagasse, Jean H. 1959. *A Study of the Population of Indian Ancestry Living in Manitoba*. 3 vols. Winnipeg: Department of Agriculture and Immigration.

Lang, John S. 1985. "Treaty No. 9 and Fur Trade Company Families." Pp. 137–62 in J. Brown and J. Peterson (eds.), *The New Peoples: Being and Becoming Métis in North America*. Winnipeg: University of Manitoba Press.

Levasseur, Donat, OMI. 1995. *Les Oblats de Marie Immaculée dans l'Ouest et le Nord du Canada, 1845–1967*. Edmonton: University of Alberta Press.

MacBeth, R.G. 1905. *Making the Canadian West*. Toronto.

McCarthy, Martha. 1987. *Pre-1870 Roman Catholic Missions in Manitoba*. Winnipeg: Historical Resources Branch Report.

Martin, Chester. 1914. "The Red River Settlement." In *Canada and its Provinces*. Vol. 19. Toronto.

——. 1920. "The First New Province of the Dominion." *Canadian Historical Review*.

Mailhot, P.R. and D.N. Sprague. 1985. "Persistent Settlers: The Dispersal and Resettlement of the Red River Métis, 1870–1885." *Canadian Journal of Ethnic Studies* 17.

McMorran, G.A. 1950. "Souris River Posts in the Hartney District." Pp. 47–62 in *Papers of the Historical and Scientific Society of Manitoba*.

McCormack, Patricia A. 1982. "Fur Trade Society to Class Society: The Development of Ethnic Stratification at Fort Chipewyan, Alberta." Vancouver: Paper presented to the CES meetings.

McCullough, Edward J. and Michael Maccagno. 1991. *Lac la Biche and the Early Fur Traders* (Occasional Publication Number 29). Edmonton: University of Alberta Press.

Mercier, Sr. Pauline. 1974. *Renseignements sur Saint-Laurent Manitoba*. Elie, MB: Division Scolaire de la Prairie du Cheval Blanc.

Morice, A. 1908. *Dictionnaire historique des Canadiens et des Métis français de l'Ouest.*.

Morton, W.L. 1937. "The Red River Parish." In R.C. Lodge (ed.), *Manitoba Essays*. Toronto: The MacMillan Co.

Mulroy, Kevin. 1993. "Ethnogenesis and Ethnohistory of the Seminole Maroons." *Journal of World History* 4: 287–305.

Nicks, Trudy and Kenneth Morgan. 1985. "Grande Cache: The Historic Development of an Indigenous Alberta Métis Population." In J. Brown and J. Peterson (eds.), *The New Peoples: Being and Becoming Métis in North America*. Winnipeg: University of Manitoba Press.

Payment, Diane. 1993. *Batoche 1870–1910*. Saint-Boniface: Les Editions du Blé.

——. 1986. "Batoche after 1885: A Society in Transition." Pp. 173–88 in F. Laurie Barron and James Waldram (eds.), *1885 and After: Native Society in Transition*. Regina: Canadian Plains Research Center.

——. 1990. *"The Free People–Otipemisiwak" Batoche, Saskatchewan 1870–1930*. Ottawa: Environment Canada.

——. 2001. "Plains Métis." Pp. 661–76 in Raymond J. DeMallie (ed.), *Plains*. Washington: Smithsonian Institution.

Pelletier, Emile. 1974. *A Social History of the Manitoba Métis*. Winnipeg: Manitoba Métis Federation Press.

Peterson, Jacqueline. 1978. "Prelude to Red River: A Social Protrait of the Great Lakes Métis." *Ethnohistory* 25 (Winter).

———. 1982. "Ethnogenesis: The Settlement and Growth of a "New People" in the Great Lakes Region, 1702–1815." *American Indian Culture and Research Journal* 6.

Proctor, Madeleine. 1960. *Woodland Echoes*. Steinbach, MB: Derksen Printers.

Rich, E.E. 1967. *The Fur Trade in the Northwest to 1857*. Toronto: McClelland and Steward Limited.

Rothney, Russ and Steve Watson. 1975. *A Brief Economic History of Northern Manitoba*. Winnipeg: Northern Planning Exercise.

Slabodin, Richard. 1981. "Subarctic Métis." In June Helm (ed.), *Subarctic*. Washington: Smithsonian Institution.

Sprague, D.N. 1972. "The Manitoba Land Question 1870–1882." *Journal of Canadian Studies* 3.

———. 1980. "Government Lawlessness in the Administration of Manitoba Land Claims, 1870–1887." *Manitoba Law Journal* 10.

———. 1981. "Métis Land Claims." (photocopy). University of Manitoba.

———. 1988. *Canada and the Métis, 1869–1885*. Waterloo: Wilfried Laurier Press.

Spry, Irene. 1985. "The Métis and Mixed Blood of Rupert's Land before 1870." Pp. 95–118 in J. Brown and J. Peterson (eds.), *The New Peoples: Being and Becoming Métis in North America*. Winnipeg: University of Manitoba Press..

Stanley, George. 1966. *The Birth of Western Canada: A History of the Riel Rebellion*. Toronto: University of Toronto Press.

Swagerty, William R.. 1980. "Marriage and Settlement Patterns of Rocky Mountain Trappers and Traders." *The Western Historical Quarterly* 7, no. 2: 159–80.

———. 1993. "A View from the Bottom Up: The Work Force of the American Fur Company on the Upper Missouri in the 1830s." *Montana The Magazine of Western History* 43: 18–33.

Thorne, Tanis C. 1996. *The Many Hands of my Relations : French and Indians on the Lower Missouri*. Columbia: University of Missouri Press.

Tough, Frank. 1996. *"As Their Natural Resources Fail": Native Peoples and the Economic History of Northern Manitoba, 1870–1930*. Vancouver: University of British Columbia Press.

———. 2000. "The Storehouses of the Good God": Aboriginal Peoples and Freshwater Fisheries in Manitoba. *Manitoba History*.

Trémaudan, Auguste-Henri de. 1935. *Histoire de la Nation Métisse de l'Ouest Canadien*. Montréal: édition Albert Levesque.

Van Kirk, Sylvia, 1980. *"Many Tender Ties": Women in the Fur Trade Society in Western Canada 1670–1870*. Winnipeg: Watson and Dwyer Publishing.

Widder Keith. 1999. *Battle for the Soul: Metis Children Encounter Evangelical Protestants at Mackinaw Mission 1823–1837*. East Lansing: Michigan University Press.

B. Theoretical and Methodological Works

Allen, V.L. 1975. *Social Analysis: A Marxist Critique and Alternative*. London and New York: Longman.

Biddiss, Michael D. 1966. "Gobineau and the Origins of European Racism." *Race* 3 (January).

Bottomore, Tom (ed.). 1983. *A Dictionary of Marxist Thought.* London: Basil Blackwell.

Brewer, Anthony. 1980. *Marxist Theories of Imperialism: A Critical Survey.* London: Routledge and Kegan Paul.

Brown, Jennifer. 1987. "People of Myth, People of History: A Look at Recent Writings on the Métis." *Acadiensis* 17: 150–62.

Clammer, John. 1985. *Anthropology and Political Economy, Theoretical and Asian Perspective.* New York: St. Martin's Press.

Hoffman, Alice. 1974. "Reliability and Validity in Oral History" *Today's Speech* 22 (Winter).

LABICA, Georges et Gérard Benoussan (eds). Dictionnaire Critique du Marxisme. Paris: Presses Universitaires de France, 1982.

Leon, Abraham. 1970. *The Jewish Question: A Marxist Interpretation.* New York: Pathfinder Press.

Lyon, M. 1972. "Race and Ethnicity in Pluralistic Societies." *New Community* 1.

Madill Dennis F.K..1988. "Riel, Red River and Beyond: New Developments in Metis History." Pp. 31–48 in Collin G. Callowah (ed.), *New Directions in American Indian History.* Norman: University of Oklahoma Press, 1988.

Magubaine, B.M. 1979. *The Political Economy of Race and Class in South Africa.* New York: Monthly Review Press.

Miles, Robert. 1980. "Class, Race and Ethnicity: A Critique of Cox's Theory." *Ethnic and Racial Studies* 3, no. 2 (April).

——. 1982. *Racism and Migrant Labour.* London: Routledge and Kegan Paul.

——. 1984. "Marxism Versus the Sociology of 'Race Relations'." *Ethnic and Racial Studies* 7 (April).

Miller, J.R. 1988. "From Riel to the Métis." *Canadian Historical Review.*

O'Laughan, Bridget. 1975. "Marxist Approaches in Anthropology." *Annual Review of Anthropology* 4.

Pannekoek, Fritz. 2001. "Metis Studies: The Development of a Field and New Directions." Pp. 111–28 in Theodore Binnema, Gerhard J. Enns and R.C. Macleod (eds.), *From Rupert's Land to Canada.* Edmonton: University of Alberta Press.

Payne, Michael. 2001. "Fur Trade Historiography: Past Conditions, Present Circumstances and a Hint of Future Prospects." Pp. 3–22 in Theodore Binnema, Gerhard J. Enns and R.C. Macleod (eds.), *From Rupert's Land to Canada.* Edmonton: University of Alberta Press.

Peterson, J. 1985. "The Indian and the Fur Trade: A Review of Recent Literature." *Manitoba History* (Spring).

Phizacklea, Annie and Robert Miles. 1980. *Labour and Racism.* London: Routledge and Kegan Paul.

Ray, A.J. 1982. "Reflections on Fur Trade Social History and Métis History in Canada." *American Indian Culture and Research Journal* 6.

St-Onge, Nicole. 1987. "Nationalist Perspectives: A Review Essay." *Manitoba History* (Autumn).

Vansine, Jan. 1965. *Oral Tradition, A Study in Historical Methodology.* London: Routledge and Kegan Paul.

Wallman, S. 1978. "The Boundaries of 'Race': Processes of Ethnicity in England." *Man* 13.

Williams, William A. 1980. "A Psychologically Justifying and Economically Profitable Fairy Tale: The Myth of Empty Continents Dotted Here and There with the Mud Huts, the Lean-Tos and the Tepees of Unruly Children Playing at Culture." In *Empire as a Way of Life*. Oxford: Oxford University Press.

Wolf, Eric R. 1982. *Europe and the People Without History*. Los Angeles: University of California Press.

C. Theses and Dissertations

Ens, Gerhard. 1989. "Kinship, Ethnicity, Class and the Red River Métis: The Parishes of St. François-Xavier and St. Andrew." PhD dissertation, University of Alberta.

Jan, H.E. 1968. "Immigration and Settlement in Manitoba, 1871-1881: The Beginnings of a Pattern." MA thesis, University of Manitoba.

Kaye, Barry. "Some Aspects of the Historical Geography of the Red River Settlement." MA thesis, University of Manitoba.

Lavallee, Guy. 1988. "The Métis People of St. Laurent, Manitoba: an Introductory Ethnography." MA thesis, University of British Columbia.

Richtik, J. M. 1964. "Historical Geography of the Interlake Area of Manitoba From 1871 to 1921." MA thesis, University of Manitoba.

Painchaud, Robert. 1976. "The Catholic Church and French Speaking Colonization in Western Canada 1885–1915." PhD dissertation, University of Ottawa.

St-Onge, Nicole J.M.1983. "Métis and Merchant Capital in Red River: The Decline of Pointe-à-Grouette 1860–1885." MA thesis. University of Manitoba.

St-Onge, Nicole J.M. 1990. "Race, Class and Ethnicity, Saint-Laurent du Manitoba, 1850-1914." PhD dissertation, University of Manitoba.

Sprenger, Herman G. 1972. "An Analysis of Selected Aspects of Métis Society 1810–1870." MA thesis, University of Manitoba.

Indexes

Subject Index

Name Index

Pangman, Marguerite (daughter of Pierre Bostonois), 11, 15
Pangman, Marguerite (née Sauteuse), 102n. 53
Pangman, Marie (daughter of Pierre Bostonois), 11
Pangman, Marie or Marguerite (née Wewejikabawik), 11, 15
Pangman, Mary (née Short), 11
Pangman, Michel, 49, 51, 77
Pangman, Napoleon, 77
Pangman, Patrice, 77
Pangman, Peter, 100n. 26
Pangman, Pierre, 26, 34, 49, 51, 77, 100n. 30, 105n. 10
Pangman, Pierre Bostonois, 11, 14, 15, 100n. 26, 102n. 53
Pangman, Pierre Jr., 11, 12, 100n. 26
Parisien, 105n. 17
Paul, St-Math, 26, 110n. 17
Peran, Father, 81
Petregum, Jules, 115n. 66
Petregum, Margaret, 115n. 66
Petregum, Mary, 115n. 66
Pritchard, 109n. 6
Pritchard, François, 44
Pritchard, Isaie, 44
Pritchard, Julie (née Boucher), 44
Provencher, Mgr., 7
R
Recourd, Louis, 112n. 5
Ressard, 109n. 6
Rey, F., 73
Richard, 33, 51, 53, 64, 74, 108n. 53, 109n. 6
Richard, François, 18, 26, 33, 51, 64, 102n. 51, 109n. 6
Richard, François Jr., 107n. 41
Richard, François Sr., 107n. 41
Richard, Isabelle (née Chartrand), 13, 64
Richard, Isaie, 51, 64
Richard, Julie (née Boucher), 64
Richard, Marguerite (née Sauteuse), 18, 51, 64, 109n. 6
Richard, Pierre, 13, 26, 51, 64
Richard, St-Pierre, 51
Riel, Louis, 28
Riel, Louis Jr., 104n. 68
Rivard, Joseph, 112n. 5
Rivard, Mary, 112n. 5
Rivard, Mary (daughter), 112n. 5
Rivard, Napoleon, 112n. 5
Robert, Geneviève, 15, 111n. 41
Rose, William, 35
S
Salomon, André, 47

Sayer, 7, 8, 17, 33, 46, 51, 53, 62, 74, 78, 102n. 53
Sayer, Baptiste, 34
Sayer, Catherine (née Pangman), 16
Sayer, Guillaume Jr., 16–17
Sayer, Guillaume Sr., 16, 17
Sayer, Jean-Baptiste, 17
Sayer, John, 17, 34
Sayer, Josephte (née Forbisher), 16
Sayer, Larose, 114n. 51
Sayer, Marie or Marguerite, 17
Sayer, Rose (née Carrière), 102n. 56
Sayer, Sarah, 114n. 51
Sayer, Suzanne (née Chartrand), 17
Sayer, Virginie, 114n. 51
Sayer, William, 102n. 56, 114n. 51
Schultz, J.C., 103n. 68
Short, Betsy (née Saulteaux), 11
Short, James, 11
Simonet, Father, 19, 20, 47, 103n. 65
Sprenger, Herman G., 11
Stevens, Louise, 14, 15
Stevens, Mary, 14, 15
T
Taché, Mgr., 18, 48, 58, 60, 61, 65
Trudel, Edmond, 57, 73
Trudel, Ernest, 113n. 13
Trudel, Georgena, 113n. 13
V
Viel, 57
Viel, Leonce, 57
Viel, Louis, 57
Viel, Margaret, 57
Viel, Mrs., 73
Viel, Raymond, 57
W
Wabikeg, Pierre, 26
Wagner, William, 30–31, 32–33, 36, 43, 51, 92, 106n. 32
Walstrom, Marie-Louise (née Lavallée), 102n. 60
Whiteford, James, 47